BEYOND CHURCH

CHURCH

The Gospel in American Life

A Collection of Works by

E. LINCOLN PEARSON

Joel Pearson, Editor

Tooliedotter Press
BELLEVUE, WASHINGTON

Beyond Church: The Gospel in American Life

Published by Tooliedotter Press LLC
P.O. Box 3544
Bellevue WA 98009-3544
http://www.tooliedotterpress.com

Corporate logo design by Studiohatch, www.studiohatch.com

All Scripture quotations are from the New Revised Standard Version Bible, copyright 1989, Division of Christian Education of the National Council of the Churches of Christ in the United States of America. Used by permission. All rights reserved.

Articles originally published in *The Covenant Companion* are reprinted here by permission of The Evangelical Covenant Church Publications.

"When Toil Is Done, a Sabbath Rest is Waiting"
Copyright 1950 by The Covenant Book Concern. Used by permission.

"Great Hills May Tremble"
"Love Divine, All Loves Excelling"
"The Spirit Breathes Upon the Word"
Copyright 1950, 1973, 1996 by Covenant Publications. Used by permission.

International Standard Book Number: 0-9747294-0-X

Printed in the United States of America

I wish to dedicate this book to my close friend, Don Frisk. He was a seminary professor for thirty-seven years, and now he joins me at the supper table nearly every day. He could have chosen to correct me with his wide knowledge of Christendom, but he does not; rather, he nurtures my flights of imagination into reasonable, usable ideas, and helps me stay within orthodoxy. To enter by conversation into that "house built on the rock" with him is to know where I can stand, and from what base I can venture forth.

❧

I would also like to dedicate the following poem to The Holmstad, a Covenant Retirement Community where I have lived for the past 11 years. Though the poem may sound like an exaggeration, I've found The Holmstad to be a wonderful place to live, and I appreciate it more with each passing year.

Holmsong

Away from the stress of the market, away from the pressured days,
Away from the hurried press of time is a cloistered, quiet place.
Nestled within is a shelter, a haven, a calm retreat,
A peace of mind the heart can find that renders the day complete.

The strain of our life is over, a music replacing the din,
The fret of our planning has run its course, changed to a joy within;
The lonely days were a passing phase, the nights of hurt are gone,
Our fears of what tomorrow brings has vanished in this dawn.

These sturdy walls do not restrain its good-will overflow,
Acquaintance leaps from name to name, that harmony may grow.
Its travel times, its good events spread wide its eager arms
To draw you to its hearty throng, enfold you with its charm.

The footsteps down the cordial hall means greeting from a friend,
And friendship, once established, is a gift that never ends.
Our meeting times transmute to joy our tales of harder years,
And loved ones, as they visit, see the end of all our fears.

When passing years shall take their toll, our frame becoming frail,
When dimming sight and lessening sound appear, and then prevail,
Then when we ask, Who cares for me? Who comes within my view?
The staffers of the Holmstad haste, each one their task to do.

For every need, that need supplied, replacing loss with gain,
For every weakening, their strength brings comfort over pain.
For each aloneness, gathered round, for every fear a prayer,
So Holmstad does enrich the lives of those who settle there.

❧

Acknowledgements

My children have produced this book; beyond the original essays it has been their work and their love that have made it possible.

Joel, as editor, has collected, selected, and organized these essays. I am deeply indebted to him for clarifying both the thought and the structure.

Mark, as a pastor, has guided my thought by demonstrating the relationship of mainstream Christianity to the new approaches I offer. In a sense, he has been the pen I write with.

Jocelyn, as publisher, has been responsible for the design, layout, printing, and distribution of this book. Her daughterly love and willingness to take on mundane but necessary tasks have made this book possible.

Melody, my eldest daughter, has been both my caretaker and encourager, keeping me willing and able to carry on. She lovingly cared for her mother during the final years of her mother's life, and she continues to provide care, encouragement, and ideas for me.

Dorothy, my late wife, has been my inspiration over these years of trying to express myself. Without the love and encouragement she has provided, I would not have been ready to say what I thought. As the Holy Spirit provides the inner sanctum in which the mind can rest in this fallen world, so Dorothy has been that dear presence by whom this life of mine has made sense.

– Lincoln Pearson

I would like to add my thanks and appreciation to McAlister Merchant for his assistance with final editing and proofing; to Dan Poynter, Marty Gilliland, and Dick Bruso for their guidance; to the reviewers whose comments helped shape the final outcome; and to our many friends who have supported us as we have brought this book to fruition.

– Jocelyn Garner, Publisher

Table of Contents

List of Poems

List of Music

Foreword

It may be tempting to try to pigeonhole Lincoln Pearson's writings, but the effort would be amiss. When he writes of the need for the faithful to be true to Christ, one is tempted to read him as only a clergyman. When he writes of the degradation of public education and public discourse, one might think of him as only a social critic. When he holds forth on ethical issues, he could be thought merely an intellectual. But there is a wit irrepressible—one moment biting in order to deflate the pompous, the next moment teasing, in order to celebrate a loved one—in order that joy might abound. And his hymns and prayers are those of a poet who whispers of glory, and sings of love that endures.

A sketch of the landscape of his life may be helpful in orienting the reader to his body of work.

Eric Edmund Lincoln Pearson was born January 27, 1917, in the small railroad town of Ashtabula, Ohio. Born to Swedish immigrants Ludwig and Frida Anderson Pearson, Lincoln grew up as the youngest of four children, knowing both economic hardship and an earnest Christian faith. Graduating from high school in the 1930's, Lincoln felt the effects of the Great Depression deeply. He was able to attend North Park College in Chicago, where he developed a reputation as a wit, and was noted for his musical ability in both voice and piano. It was at North Park College and Seminary that he produced some of his best early work.

His pursuit of higher education would continue throughout most of the rest of his adult life. Not content with completing junior college and seminary, he also earned a Bachelor of Arts from Saint Anselm College, completed additional studies at Tarkio College, earned a Masters in Education from Northern Illinois University, and accumulated a total of 300 undergraduate and graduate semester hours—the natural result of his long-standing interest in the interaction of Christianity and the Public Square.

The first phase of Lincoln Pearson's adult life centered on ministry: Seminary at North Park, pastorates in New Hampshire, Minnesota, Iowa, and Wisconsin. The second phase placed him in public education. In 1959, at the age of 42, Lincoln moved his family to Illinois where he became a public school teacher. For the next 23 years he taught English and Social Studies at the Junior High and Middle School levels. This experience provided the front row seat from which he could observe first hand the changes in the character of the typical student; eroding from self-discipline to self-absorption, from respect to rebellion.

The third phase, retirement, is filled with a quiet flurry of activity, born from desire to prove useful, to add value to his community wherever possible. Retiring from teaching at the age of 65, Lincoln was not content to sit back and let the world go by. For years he volunteered once a week at local nursing homes. He played and sang popular music and songs of faith the residents would know and love. He immersed himself in the work of his local congregation, and eventually found himself on staff there as part-time visitation pastor. He retired from that only when he and his wife, Dorothy, moved from the family home to a Covenant retirement community in Batavia, Illinois. There his efforts to better the world close at hand continued unabated.

It seems that there were always two special places in Lincoln's home, his workshop and his study (which came to be known affectionately as his "monastery"). From each came products essential, original, and memorable. Carpentry for Lincoln has always been for him an opportunity to create—not for mere self-expression but to provide solutions both clever and cost-effective. In their home in Illinois he crafted for Dorothy a kitchen and pantry that featured hidden drawers, efficient storage, and ingenious work surfaces. In retirement his projects have benefitted a broad range of people, private and public, friends close at hand, and his community at large.

Over the course of his adult life, Lincoln Pearson has produced an estimated 1,100 writings: articles, letters to the editor, hymns, prayers, poems, essays and commentaries of various sorts. Many of these were in the form of weekly commentaries on Scripture and daily life produced for one congregation or another. One series was called "Pearson's Parables," and another was "Linc Thinks." But because of his focus on the message and not on the messenger, Linc gave no thought to preserving or publishing these for a wider audience. It was enough, in his mind, to further the Kingdom and not feather the cap.

It has only been in recent years that he has given any thought to publishing a collection of his written work, and then only at the consistent urging of family and friends. His hope in publishing these writings now is like the intent of his woodworking, that in some small way careful craftsmanship freely offered might bless a world in need of putting back together.

As you examine and engage what follows, we trust you will sense a resemblance in these pages between Lincoln Pearson's workmanship and that of the Carpenter he serves.

– Mark Pearson
December 2003

Preface

Shortly before she passed away, Lincoln's wife, Dorothy, was reminded that her husband was about to be a published author. When asked what she thought of that idea, she grinned and replied quietly, "That's OK, as long as it doesn't go to his head."

Dorothy needed not have been concerned: if anything, Lincoln Pearson is modest to a fault. His humility is exceeded only by his passion for the Gospel, which has been the guiding light throughout his life and is evidenced within the chapters of this book. Though the writings in this book span a period of 65 years, the themes are consistent:

- That Jesus Christ is Lord of all.
- That a personal decision and an individual relationship with Christ are the prerequisites for salvation and a godly life, and result in a change of character accomplished by the indwelling of the Holy Spirit.
- That devotion to Jesus Christ and service to others are the traits which flow naturally from the Holy Spirit's work in our lives.
- That our faith should be applied to our lives outside the church walls, including describing our faith to unbelievers.

It is this last point that prompted the compilation of this book from Lincoln's vast collection of essays and other material. When asked why he wanted to write a book, Lincoln commented that "the average churchgoer is almost helpless in defending and describing their faith to unbelievers." In particular, Lincoln's essays attempt to show the thought process for applying one's faith in everyday life. He has a good variety of examples for readers to ponder as they consider the state of their own walk with Jesus Christ.

There are articles and essays in this book that manifest a concern about the deterioration of American society because of a lack of recognition of the country's Christian roots. There is also a suggestion that the influence of Christ peaked somewhere around the early part of the 20th century. Furthermore, said influence appears to have been steadily declining, as measured by the drop in church attendance in the last few decades and the increasing emphasis on individual needs over the health and well-being of the Body of Christ.

Some of the seeds of that decline were sown in the church itself by focusing on external evidence of "success." As long as there were plenty of people in the pews, everything was OK, but in reality, few churches were following up with those churchgoers to determine the depth of their commitment to Jesus Christ, and to help disciple them.

Christian influence has been declining according to these common measurements, but more subtle and positive influences are often overlooked. Christian values were written into American laws by the founding fathers, and those values continue to hold the society together to a degree. The tragic events of recent years have rekindled an interest in faith and patriotism, and comprehending the fragility of life has caused many to return to the faith of their youth. While we are not advocating faith in Jesus Christ as "fire insurance," these events have provided a fresh opportunity for a dialogue about Him as Lord and Savior, and this book is certainly intended to enhance and promote that discussion.

Towards that end, the author is encouraging the use of this book as a source for discussions in churches and at home. Copyright fair-use laws permit the copying of *portions* of this book for study purposes, and Lincoln wholeheartly supports readers who want to make fair-use photocopies as they examine this book in Sunday School and or in small groups.

It is our prayer that this book will bring fresh insights into the love of Jesus Christ, His impact on our way of life, and the His ultimate triumph over sin and death. For further information about this book and resources for further study, please see the web site, http://www.beyondchurch.com.

– Joel Pearson, Editor
– Jocelyn Garner, Publisher

Introduction: A Note from Linc

1997. This cover letter was sent to 7 sibling households with selections included in this book.

I know it is presumptuous of me to send you these pages of my ramblings, in the hope that you will read them. But listen to my story.

For a couple of years now, I have had this obsession, which is that those who profess Christianity need to see more of the whole picture than most do; that the personal faith they hear about and practice is not a sufficient portion of the whole truth; that the aspects which deal with the nation as a whole are vital. This national aspect has first interested me, then bothered me. But I have had no outlet for it, no one to listen to me.

Then a week ago I had the chance to read this paper to the Holmstad clergy meeting. Their reply was astounding; they not only liked it; they discussed it far beyond their usual closing time. And at the end, they gave it a standing ovation — applause well beyond the usual limits. (I think they were getting to their feet anyway.)

Not that the paper was well written; it was not. Not the messenger, but the message. But that I was discussing something vital - that was their impression. I didn't sleep much last night, and in the middle of the night it dawned on me: I have something that some understand, but most don't. That amounts to a responsibility given to me; I'm supposed to tell it somehow.

How, I don't know. If God is involved in this, He will find a way. It's awfully late in life for me. Maybe in years to come, someone will take up the banner.

The point of this whole page is this: I feel my obsession has been vindicated. Like the woman in the parable who found the lost coin, I had to tell someone about it, and you were elected. Thanks for listening.

– Linc

Part I:
American Life

Chapter 1:
The Path of a Nation

This chapter directly addresses American culture and values, and the impact of Christianity in the development of the nation and its future.

My Covenant with God

April 1962. *Written while Lincoln was teaching middle school.*

Our fathers, from a distant land,
Approached in faith this blessed shore,
They heard the voice of Christ's command,
To follow as in days of yore.
So on this holy ground, by grace,
I vow that where their feet have trod,
I too shall walk, and seek His face.
This is my covenant with God!

My days, my mortal powers, my thought,
And all the motives of my soul,
I yield to Christ the Lord, who bought
My freedom from sin's cruel control
My heart, whene'er I hear his voice,
With gratitude is overawed —
This is the gospel I must send,
This is my covenant with God!

As evil teachings hold their power,
Deluding victims of the night,
We rally to the Lord this hour,
To Him who is the truth, the light.
May his transforming mercy lend
The strength to shed his love abroad –
This is the gospel I must send,
This is my covenant with God!

❧

Members of Each Other

1983. *Written shortly after Lincoln retired from teaching.*

So deeply we are bound to one another!
We try to flee the burden of belonging;
We turn away from those we do not like,
But there they are again in days that follow.
Often then they have us at a disadvantage.
The wife who leaves her husband, wanting freedom
Must call in panic for the plumber late at night;
The husband says good riddance, but so soon
He burns the eggs he fries in some small lonely room.
The small boy screams in anger at his friend
But next day needs a catcher for his team.
The social climber snubs the druggist's wife,
But getting refills for her pills she sees her there.
That no-good boy-friend of your precious daughter
Tomorrow joins the company-- your boss's nephew.
The school-girl sneered at by the "in" crowd
Would offer help to pass the next exam.
The college lad who thinks his folks are dumb
Falls hopelessly behind in payments on his car.
The sneering braggart who would often taunt police
Until some driver, hit-and-run, then knocks him down.
The vain physician thinks you are an object, nothing more,
Must watch his father die by inches, with no cure.
And he who trusted no one over thirty,
Has now in years just come to thirty-one.
The neighbor who would never stop and talk
Now needs a ride to the emergency room.
He who robbed you last year in that car repair
Is diagnosed as having terminal leukemia.
The rich man, so secured behind high fences,
Was found today. A heart attack. He was alone.

She was supremely beautiful and proud
Until one side of her facelift swelled.
The girl who quit her school (it was a prison)
Now has three children, and a drunken husband.
That business man, so clever, never home,
Returned. His only child is mongoloid.
My friend who always reads the Wall Street Journal
Lost everything he had-- a "sure thing" in the market.
Freedom? Independence? No such thing.
We are members of each other, bound together
By the love of God, and by our awful need
For someone who will love and care, unworthy as we are.
Beloved, let us love each other.
❧

Jesus and the Moral Vacuum

June 15, 1983. *This article originally appeared in The Covenant Companion.*

The United States of America was organized under a unique premise, that its citizens would have sufficient integrity and honesty of character to carry out the duties of citizenship with a minimum of external controls. In effect, our forebears assumed that everyone could be trusted. To the rest of the world this was a foolhardy, even insane supposition. Alexis de Tocqueville, a French philosopher, decried the Constitution as being "all sails, no anchor." Too many rights, not enough duties. Too many freedoms, not enough safeguards. Abraham Lincoln, at Gettysburg, wondered "whether that nation, or any nation so conceived and so dedicated, can long endure."

The Constitution of the United States has been copied in whole or in part by many countries in the past two hundred years. And most have failed miserably; their elections have become mockeries, their presidents have become dictators, and the inner workings of their governments have been snowed under by a tide of bribery and corruption. Marxist countries, it appears, deliberately operate on the assumption that no one can be trusted. In retrospect, our trust in the goodness of humanity appears to have been both naive and foolhardy.

But it has worked. Why? I am convinced it is because there has been enough Christian influence and Christian conscience in our country to make this trust-me system work passably well. Though the motives of many of our public servants have been lamentable, enough of the spirit of Jesus has seeped through to hold the fabric of society together.

Now, however, it is apparent to us all that public integrity is not strong enough, our trust-me system is too vulnerable, and conniving is breaking public trust. Prosecution of wrongdoers has been of no help. Any society periodically "throws the rascals out," but usually the replacement turns out to be no better.

What force is there that produces character, promoting the ideals and loyalties that hold a society together? I know of none other than God himself, as shown to us in Jesus Christ. Whether he comes to us by inspiration inwardly or reproach outwardly, whether by the love of parents or the warning of the law, whatever the vehicle or form, we have one source — Jesus Christ. And that influence can go remarkably far beyond those who confess his name. When the atheist claims that his civil rights have been violated, he claims a standard based on Jesus.

In fact, the teachings of Jesus have served as a standard for the ethical structure of our nation. Not that they have been obeyed, but they have served as a measure by which to compare our actions. The continuing cry for civil rights assumes that each person is of infinite value, that every life is precious, that our rights are not to be hampered by poverty, and that government has a duty to protect these rights. All of these assumptions come from the New Testament, and hold true only to the extent that Jesus and his teachings are respected. Can you imagine that kind of clamor in a country without God? Can you imagine the women of Islamic nations arguing successfully against sex discrimination?

But now the concept of Christianity as a tool of ethical measure is fading out. Our judicial system is getting confused. Lacking an accompanying moral sense to validate our laws, judges frequently contradict themselves, strain at the gnat and swallow the camel. Appeal to a higher court produces a good chance for reversal. As without gravity there is no up and down, so without Christ as standard the sense of what is good and what is evil is lost.

I listened recently to a few soap operas, and felt distressed without knowing why at first. Then I realized that I felt no ethical framework; that the discussions referred to no standard. The characters spoke in a moral vacuum. Without a sense of right and wrong their make-believe tribulations made no sense at all.

Jesus has also served as the conscience of our nation. Criminals used to be ashamed of what they had done, but now they are interviewed on TV, where they explain that there was nothing wrong with their behavior. Most of our public officials once did their duty because of an unspoken understanding that the highest kind of life gives itself without reservation to its task, and that we all must follow that example. In many other governments it is assumed that the shepherd will steal from the flock and manipulate laws for personal gain. Now it is happening here also. We are losing faith in the workability of our system; there is simply not enough integrity to go around.

Government efforts to provide for the needy have been based on that national conscience. But there is so much fraud in the food stamp program that it has become more a means of theft than of mercy. In the collection of the income tax, cheating is so substantial that another, less trusting system may have to be found. In control of crime, there was a time when the fact that a murder had been committed was not obscured by legal maneuvering; our conscience was the deciding factor. But without that conscience, even a movie of the crime being committed might not convince a jury.

The national conscience has also weakened considerably in the use of money. The Scriptures insist that we must not steal, and as individuals we agree. But government itself, which should be the enforcer of national honesty, has convinced us that by some slight of hand we can spend more than we earn, we can have that which we have not worked for, and that we really do not owe anything for that which we have wasted. It sounds almost like we have accepted what the serpent said in the Garden of Eden: "You will not die..." (*Genesis 3:4*).

Even the Christian community has not expressed the qualms, the uneasiness we sense about accepting what we have not earned. "The serpent tricked me, and I ate," (*Genesis 3:13*) we say. But payment in one form or another is surely coming due. "Where did you get that dollar?" asks the parent. "I found it," replies the youngster. But the parent will not be satisfied with that answer; and in the cosmic scheme of things, neither will God.

Without continuous renewal of the moral sense, we lose the vertical dimension in life. As conscience fades, nothing seems very wrong, and nothing very right. It becomes a two-dimensional world, where decisions are made with the flip of a coin. Evil shows up as evil only in a strong God-presence.

Jesus has also served our country well as a motivator. He is the only adequate answer to the question, "Why?" Without belief in an ultimate and triumphant justice there is no reason to do the difficult and honorable thing. If the rewards for decent behavior are at best capricious and at worst grossly unfair, why should I try? If there is no basic righteousness that reigns supreme, there is no point in doing the kind or unselfish thing. "Why should I make the effort to learn?" "Why should I obey the traffic laws?" "Why should I be honest about my income tax?" "Why shouldn't I cheat to get ahead?" The deeds that hold a society like ours together make sense only if there is in our minds the concept of a holy and loving God. The Apostle Paul said it best: "If Christ has not been raised, your faith is futile and you are still in your sins." (*1 Corinthians 15:17*).

Vandalism, they say, is an expression of rage against the hopelessness of existence without meaning. Signs of that kind of rage are increasing. When the influence of Jesus fades, might becomes more important than right and our whole system f government enters the crisis stage. If it can no longer count on the integrity of s citizens, it has no choice but to become harsh, arbitrary, and without chance appeal.

Patrick Henry, in his speech to the Virginia House of Burgesses, defined our ecessary reliance: "Besides, sir, we fight not our battles alone. There is a just God, ho presides over the destinies of nations." The psalmist said it this say: "Unless ne Lord guards the city, the guard keeps watch in vain." (*Psalms 127:1*). We must ll again on Jesus to be the Savior of our free society; unless he can rule kindly om within, we shall be ruled by others harshly from without. ❧

We Drift

1981. *Written shortly before Lincoln retired from teaching.*

The luxury liner America, on its annual cruise, miscalculated its course ar
was forced to pass through that area of the World Sea called Desperation Triang
that part bounded by the islands of Poverty, Disease, and Famine. Usually th
avoided that part of the sea because picking up survivors often caused them to g
far behind schedule, to the irritation of many of the passengers.

This time the unthinkable happened; the America collided with another sh
called World Need. The accident was not considered serious at first, but th
inexorable sinking at the bow finally convinced the passengers that they must ta
to the lifeboats.

There was a good deal of confusion in the loading — who would go first, ho
much they could bring with them, along with a lot of cursing about whose fault
was. Finally after several accidents the boats were loaded.

I was in Number 77, so I can tell you what took place there. When th
indignation was finally under control, we noticed that some of the other lifeboa
were from the other ship, the World Need. We tried to signal them to give us hel
but none came close.

Night came on, and it became bitterly cold. The people huddled together f
warmth — sometimes neighbors they had never met. The boats were large, ve
old-fashioned (since they were never intended to be used) made of wood, wi
high sides.

Someone took a metal suitcase away from an old woman and started a fire
it. Many wanted to warm themselves, but there was nothing to use for fuel. O
enterprising person tore away the top board on one side, had plenty of help to g
it broken into pieces, and it was added to the fire.

Others moved toward the warmth, and the boat tipped precariously. It w
moved, seconded, and carried that the other top boards should also be added
the fire, and they were.

Someone objected that we must not lower the sides of the boat that way - th
in high waves the boat could readily sink. But the comfort people won out. Eve

ıree hours the top board - or whatever remained as the top board - would be
dded to the fire, and we moved in orderly fashion to warm ourselves in turn.

The sea is calm now, but we are down to about six inches above the waterline...
'o find out what happens, you and I must wait for tomorrow... ❧

Chaos or Tyranny: America's Dilemma

July 1, 1979. *This article originally appeared in the issue of The Covenant Companion.*

As an amateur painter paints himself into a corner, with the walls convergin behind him and no place to go, so America finds itself between two convergin forces with no outlet, no solution in sight. These forces are the increasing amour of government regulation on the one hand and the overemphasis on individu rights on the other. Carried to their extremes we could label them tyranny versu chaos.

It would appear that since these are opposites, the common sense positio would be halfway between them, but this is not necessarily the case. Already the have met; already they overlap in some aspects. And it is a struggle that appea on many levels.

When an individual complains of the lack of police vigilance at one momen and of police harassment in the next breath, he wants more freedom for himse and more regulation for his neighbor. In local government the official says, i effect, "Give me your money and trust me," while the citizen joins a group to a as watchdog over his tax money to ensure that the expenditures will be honest an prudent. One party calls for more freedom, the other for more control.

In planning the long-range security of our land the argument seesaws bac and forth: We cannot just saunter blithely into the future while the Sovie are obviously planning our downfall; we must have the draft and more cove intelligence-gathering operations, more vigilance. No, is the reply; if we must li in fear and do without our vacations, then we have lost the very thing we plan guard — our freedom.

But it is in the relationships between the federal government and the citize that our dilemma comes into clearest focus. It is significant that the law-enforcin agencies of the government consider cheating and theft so enormous a phenomeno that they plan no moves against it, considering it hopeless to solve. Score a big o for chaos. Federal agencies are making and interpreting rules that have extensiv repercussions in our private lives. Score a big one for tyranny. In criminal law, th rights of the accused far outweigh the rights of the victim-another blow by chao In the matter of discrimination there are signs that we are guilty until we can prov that we are innocent-reversal of the usual concept and a gain for tyranny. If th

overnment would make some more free, it must do so at the cost of regulating
nd restricting others. I heard a friend say, "If this keeps up, we are going to be
o free and equal that nobody will be able to move." This is what I mean by the
verlap; chaos and tyranny mix together in the same problems.

But there is a way out. For the people who walk in this growing darkness there
indeed a great light. Our first clue appears when we realize that the failings
e describe in the government are really those found in every individual. Face
: we are saying, "Let me go ahead but hold them back. Give me my rights, but
ie other person needs to be corrected. Give me my sacred privacy, but we must
f course pry into our neighbor's nefarious doings. I'm carrying too much of the
nancial load, but he's getting off too easy."

This warped view of the universe that puts us at the center, this extreme bias in
vor of ourselves that makes us the angel and the other fellow the villain, is simply
riginal sin given full rein and lacking originality. This is why our jobs never pay
1ough for what we do, while some mindless entertainer makes thousands more.
this why the boss seems to watch us and the clock so carefully, while other
nployees seem to roam freely? Do tyranny and chaos both begin in us? They do,
1d they are so intermingled that we cannot find the golden mean between them.
Vhile self is paramount, there will never be enough freedom for us and never
ifficient restriction on the other person. It is hard for us to acknowledge the "... I
) the very thing I hate." (*Romans 7:15*) spirit in ourselves, which turns liberty so
isily into license and control into tyranny.

So America's problem is basically a spiritual one. If this is true, why does it seem
ore crucial in this decade than before? Several reasons. We are crowding together
ore rapidly now. Our natural resources, heretofore in endless supply, are found
› be limited. So our fallen nature tells us that we must get our share-there is a
ace of panic in the air-and we plead with the powers that be to allow us to be
rst in line.

But the principal reason for our accelerating crisis is that our self-restraint
1d self-control have weakened to the point where they are overridden by our
issions. For a generation now we have been playing down traditional values. For
generation there has been a deadly silence about decency and right and wrong in
ur classrooms, and the results are plain to see.

Malcolm Muggeridge, the English journalist, is right when he describes ou Western civilization as running in the "Gadarene Stakes," likening us to th demoniacs who entered a herd of swine and then rushed down the steep bank t deliberately destroy themselves. (*Matthew 8:28-34*)

No doubt there have been societies and cultures in which the two opposin forces have been held at stalemate, with little clash between them. It is axiomati that freedom for the individual should exist to the extent that his behavior doc not harm his neighbor and that government should intervene only when does. But this seldom happens. Most of the governments on our planet intrud unnecessarily far into the lives of their citizens, limiting them beyond what necessary. Dictators tend not to take chances. Tyranny is more comfortable an more permanent than chaos.

But we were meant for something better than a balance of forces. One way t describe the effect of salvation (and this is a very limited interpretation) is to sa that the presence of Christ produces an inner imperative which diminishes th need for external controls. In him, the fence is inside; his Spirit makes many outc barriers unnecessary. No one needs to watch the coats in the church foyer becaus we assume that those present have inner compulsions that make theft unthinkabl Conversely, it is the lack of inner restraints in the call for freedom that causes mo and more outward regulation of our lives. As the inner fences fail, more outwar fences appear.

In another sense Christ is not a part of the battle between opposing forces. H is neither tyranny nor chaos, nor an arbiter between them. In fact, belief in hi opens a space between them that is true liberty. His love constrains, but it does nc restrain. He is a dynamic, a direction, and not a barrier.

Those who now live under oppressive regimes and have found Christ are radiai as they describe the freedom he gives. Even before his influence begins to bear o their society they realize he is the way. They see him as a rising sun.

As for us, living in a land where his influence seems to be waning, we loo with sorrow at a government which adds a few more rules each day just tryin to protect us from one another. It looks as though we are running out of tha precious ingredient which makes our kind of society possible. In the words of tł old German proverb, we threw out the baby with the bath water; the influence c the Christian religion, even at a remote distance, was much greater than we ha

ispected. His salvation held decency and respect and responsibility and honesty
1 place: as Paul writes to the Colossians, "...in him all things hold together."
Colossians 1:17)

There is no way, short of Christ, that we are going to recapture the solidity of
tizenry that gave us elbow room. Each new decision, no matter which way it
ans, will only add to the thicket of rules and to our frustration. No system of
hics will do it. We can all describe an ideal society; we all know what is right.
ut until Jesus dwells in us we shall feel deprived, and we shall covet what is our
eighbor's; we shall be afraid, and we shall plot to limit our neighbor's freedom in
1e vain hope that his increasing bondage will mean our growing liberty. ❧

Chapter 2:
Public Education

The selections in this chapter discuss the application of one's faith while functioning in the public school system.

O Hamilton, My Hamilton

1970. *To the tune of O Tannenbaum. A humorous look at daily life at Hamilton Junior High School in Loves Park, Illinois, where Lincoln taught.*

O Hamilton, my Hamilton, your halls are awful crowded.
The narrow-minded may slip through; the broad of beam are routed.
The locker door may hide the face,
The rest protrudes, and blocks the space.
O Hamilton, my Hamilton, your halls are awful crowded.

O Hamilton, my Hamilton, your athletes are splendid.
They train by running up the stairs, and down the halls till winded.
One year we won three games or more,
But that was when we kept the score.
O Hamilton, my Hamilton, your athletes are splendid.

O Hamilton, my Hamilton, a teacher's inspiration.
For after this, no other job could bring us perspiration.
And when you've taught three years or more,
You wouldn't mind atomic war,
O Hamilton, my Hamilton, a teacher's inspiration.

❧

Sneers Produce Ignorance

1985. *Printed in the Rockford Register-Star, Rockford, Illinois.*

To the Editor:

Public education's request for a bigger budget is understandable, but it is beside the point. Parochial and Christian private schools are doing a better job with less than half the money, less educated teachers, less materials and supplies, and less attractive environments. Why such a gap in performance?

What public school systems need is something money cannot buy – the student's attitude. Religious schools place great importance on the right attitude, for it is the key to motivation, as any parent can tell you. The motives that make for efficient learning are those based on our traditional values:

A sense of security from parents who love and encourage; willing acceptance of a required standard of conduct; respect for elders and teachers; recognition of the privilege of attending school; a sense of duty, and responsibility fitting one's level of maturity; pride in our country, and belief in a divine presence who holds us responsible for our actions.

These attitudes are laughed at as being hopelessly square and out-of-date. But it is that very cynicism that makes learning itself seem foolish; our scoffing makes us unable to bend to the task. Too many children are victims of sneers taught them by adults, and it is hard for them to believe in anything. This "jeer and sneer" syndrome makes the teacher's task difficult if not impossible.

In lower grades many good values still persist, but in the higher grade derision, scorn, and contempt appear, usually disguised as "cool," as sophistication — inferring that one is above all that is offered. I was a public school teacher for many years, and I saw open eagerness change slowly to sullen disdain, expecting rights without duties, privilege without responsibility, success without work, and promotion without trying.

Public school teachers are doing their best, but the tide is against them. Our cynical society becomes the victim of its own debunking. ❧

The Life of Lyle Preston:
Tampering With the Grades

1999. *Originally published on the Internet.*

Lyle Preston pulled his car into a slot at the school's parking lot, turned it off, and headed toward the building. On his way from home he had been thinking about the news article about grades, particularly the ones at Madison Junior High.

Heading toward Room 13, he met Roger Abbott, the principal. "Say, Roge, I noticed the news report about our grades. We did well; better than I thought we had. Why the difference?"

With a slightly embarrassed grin, Roger answered, "There was an improvement in the grades, wasn't there. You see, the grades for the public take in the expectations of the parents; we don't want to disappoint them."

"The grades differ according to the person looking at them?"

"Well, we thought it was best to leave off the grades of those who are adversely affected in retention of facts; that's Ben's and Lily's rooms. That's fairer than having them compete with those in other categories; they are encouraged by this report."

"That would pep them up; they are not losers at all! But then the grade is not a measure, it's a hopeful prediction."

On to Room 13. Thought Lyle, These kids who work hard are getting cheated this way, you can win without trying. If there is no losing, then there is no winning either. If the truth ever gets out, somebody's going to have to answer for this.

The truth in our time is just to hard for us to face; the pretending is easier to bear. Maybe it's a part of American thinking; there must be progress, we must be successful, better today than yesterday. We know more than they did years ago; therefore our decisions must look brighter.

The school day must be a little shorter; the grind of the classroom must be punctuated with lighter moments. The alone work should give way to working together with another student, which includes conversation. We've seen it in college schedules: shorter school year, more breaks, less time in class, subjects considered in a course include more trivial stuff, but defended with plenty of educationese, insisting that this is a more efficient way to learn.

Lyle felt that he was affected by this trend; the maps can wait until next Tuesday, and you draw not from scratch, but from an outline provided. He felt guilty in yielding that way, but who cares? He hated himself for that thought.

"I'll never cover Algeria this way. And I bet that no other teacher would complain about the rise in grades. Are we putting up a facade, and keeping silent about those who simply aren't trying?"

How deep is this evasion? Are we talking original sin? Isn't laziness a universal failing? And isn't the wish of the parent that Johnny learn all that is presented? ❧

The Life of Lyle Preston:
The Promotion

1999. *Originally published on the Internet.*

Mike Bailey was a seventh grader who refused to be frightened into studying. He was like that in all of his classes. His teachers sent a letter home at mid-year, telling his parents that Mike was doing nothing. There was no reply from the Baileys, but it was assumed that the message had been received; Mike said he brought it home.

The stalemate continued throughout the school year; the teachers no longer implored Mike to study; it was no use. But when there were only six weeks left in the second semester, the principal phoned his mother and asked her to meet with the teachers. She came. The principal and Mike's teachers met with her.

This time the teachers had an ultimatum: Unless Mike studied during these last six weeks, he would not be promoted. This had some effect; Mike agreed to study the remaining time. And study he did, a week or so, but that's all.

The teachers met again: shall Mike be promoted? Of course he did not deserve it, but should he be allowed to punish his teachers by being in their classes again? And a more weighty argument: Would it do Mike any good for him to take the seventh grade over again? No teacher wanted him. So the decision was: let him be promoted, since it would do him no good to stay.

Those of us who consider this from a distance and from elapsed time are disgusted with that decision. But the teachers saw it logically: Why punish the boy since it would do no good?

From this distance we can see that they did not consider the whole problem: what about its effect on the rest of the school? It tells them that studying is optional; this boy defied them and was promoted. To solve a small dilemma they created a massive problem, one that could last for years.

Check the motives involved: those that had responsibility did not carry it out; those who had a task did not do it; the blame was placed on other people. No one in the group took on the task; it would wait until some other teacher discovered that Mike could not do the simplest task. And he or she, seeing the problem was now more unsolvable, would also pass Mike along.

This has happened a thousand times, till Mike and those like him graduated from high school without being able to read. The cumulative weight of all these boys and girls unable to read has produced a reaction: no more social promotions. The idea has reached government, laws have been passed, principals chastened, and the debacle about Mike can no longer happen.

When we refuse to obey, life gets tangled. We tried freedom anyway; that didn't work. Now we try imprisonment; stay where you are until you obey. Neither will do; there must come a new spirit that does not constrain, but says "Come." ❧

The Life of Lyle Preston:
Shall We Strike?

1999. *Originally published on the Internet.*

Lyle Preston came upon another crisis in his teaching career - a strike. The teachers felt that they should be paid more, and so at the beginning of the school year they refused to come into the buildings to begin their work.

Why did they feel they should be paid more? Several reasons appeared: Some other school district nearby had a higher pay scale, and so to be fair, our district should pay as much. I doubt that any reference was made to need; they could get along on what they were getting. But every person feels they are worth more than they really are, so the cry for more, though it is plain selfishness, finds some reason which sounds reasonable. They may not have thought of it themselves, but from somewhere there will come a story that will pass muster: the one teacher whose house burned down, and is now in great debt; the teacher whose wife has been at death's door, and needs help with the hospital bills; the professionalism of the job requires more respect than the present wage can suffice; the four or five years of college were extremely difficult, which people don't realize.

The three months in which they do not work, but have other jobs, are not discussed. The average annual wage of a teacher is not limited to what the school district pays; most have summer jobs which produce a decent wage.

So when the school days are to begin, the teachers are there, but they are standing outside, manning the picket line. They are backed by the National Education Association, a very strong union.

Lyle showed up, but he walked into the building for work. There were numerous catcalls, and it meant that some teachers would no longer be his friends. There would be tense moments in the teachers' lounge.

Lyle felt that he was well paid, and his conscience would not let him join. One of the older men asked him why he was so stubborn. Not that he would change his mind, but it might help somehow. If we were to condense his thinking, it would something like this:

The purpose of a teacher is to teach, and thereby serve the community. Serving with even a sacrificial ideal is inherent in the philosophy of teaching. If this job is seen as taking from the community more than it gives, it should be ashamed. The public schools are an extension of a community's love for its children; we teach and we provide money to teach because we love. This is a Christian idea; that we are willing to pay to have someone else's child learn is no common sense; it is an exalted idea. But making teaching very profitable changes its spirit; we begin to rob the community rather than serve it.

To strike at the beginning of the school year is to take advantage when the district is most vulnerable. The teachers always win, and their salaries go up. This can be repeated every year if they wish. Salaries can rise far beyond what the job is really worth, to become a heavy load on a community. This is a shame. ❧

Is The Child Safe?

1998. *Originally published on the Internet.*

Since it is apparent that parochial schools and Christian schools do a better job of teaching boys and girls, and yet no one seems to know why, I offer these ideas as coming from Christianity, in the hope that they can be used in public school situations, thereby hopefully raising the standards wherever they appear. Here are the seven questions each child asks his-or-her self on entering the classroom.

1. **Am I Safe?** No child can adequately face life without some safeguards, most of which are supplied by the parents. Years ago, the teacher seemed to be like a grandmother, or an aunt, someone from whom safety emanated. The child of 80 years ago basked in that security; today the dangers are many. The idea of a God who loved us strengthened that feeling.

2. **Am I Loved?** When both parents work and have little time to spend with their child, it is a serious question. With several children, some may feel left out. If the parents are particularly success-minded, there is even less time, and less love. Does the classroom represent love, or does the commotion rule it out? Those children who also go to church can better carry that aura with them; come what may, God loves them.

3. **Am I Valuable?** If the grades are so-so or low, who seems to care? Does the teacher make that clear, to even Loretta who is shabbily dressed? That nobody cares will shut down the mind, and often the child will hide away crushed by the knowledge that nobody cares. The Bible helps this a lot; "All are precious in His sight" is great comfort.

4. **Why Shall I Obey?** That there is an all-good, all-wise, all-loving authority above us — that is clear to the child who goes to church. But what the child sees and hears in the classroom may contradict that; authority that surrenders to a spoiled child's whims, and language not appropriate for their ears. If there is no outside reassurance, obedience falls prey to what someone else is getting away with.

5. **Are My Efforts Necessary?** In our world of topsy-turvy values, the will to work hard is less persuasive than it used to be. Sports beckon as possible easy money; drugs make working by the hour look foolish; marrying

someone rich seems to be an easy road. The student must be absolutely convinced that the drudgery of learning is the only way to go. We are doing a poor job of persuading.

6. **Will My Eventual Reward Be Proportional To My Efforts?** Those at the top of the class are sure of it; their parents show them how. But the marginal student thinks of the effort as wasted or futile; My Dad did O.K. and I'll get a good job, you just see. The goal must be in sight.

7. **What of the Future?** A turbulent world, unstable parents, a growing rebellion, a poor attendance record, and enemies appearing: None of us know the future.

But they who believe in God have a hold on it; God rules and God cares. That's why the religion-based school does better. ❧

hrist and Culture: The Public Schools

arch 15, 1974. *This article originally appeared in The Covenant Companion.*

It was dismaying to read in a December issue of Christianity Today that anscendental Meditation, which author David Haddon sees as a variant Hinduism, has made amazing inroads into institutions of higher learning our country, and is even being taught in some high schools. The federal vernment recently provided a grant for the training of 130 high school teachers Transcendental Meditation. The Illinois House of Representatives has passed resolution encouraging its study in all educational institutions. More than a ousand colleges now have chapters of the Student's Transcendental Meditation ciety.

Part of the reason for this phenomenal growth and its entrance into many tax-pported schools is its insistence that it is not a religion but a science. It claims to oduce a number of benefits, including the reducing of addiction to drugs. But e searching article in Christianity Today leaves no doubt that it is a religion.

The fact that this teaching has walked in easily where institutional Christianity s for so long knocked at the door should jolt the complacency of Christian lucators. It will also crush our belief that the public-supported school is a iritually neutral buffer zone in which we agree to keep the peace by not trying propagate our beliefs.

The truth is that the public school is not spiritually neutral. It is definitely stile. Its climate tends to quench the faith, belittle the ideal, and label devotion fanaticism. Unless spiritual forces outside the school intervene, we should not surprised to find that a student's cynicism increases proportionately with his ars in the public school.

A glance at a typical curriculum shows that God is effectively excluded. In the udy of science, apparently complex forms of life evolved from the simpler without eding a pervading intelligence and power to make the changes. Mathematics andles the precision of the universe without seeing the cause behind the ganization and order throughout. The language courses stress communication a tool, but do not ask for what end it is used. History rehearses the follies of ations and societies without realizing that there is an inherent weakness in the ature of man that cancels out its utopias.

27

Twelve years or more of student exposure to this kind of climate rules out for many the probability that "in Him we live and move and have our being." (*Acts 1* 28) At best, religion is given a small compartment, caricatured, and effectively insulated from influencing behavior.

The crux of our dilemma seems to lie in our definition of religion. We have traditionally held that religion is a belief in a personal God. It is with the assumption that we have claimed our tax exemptions, our discounts, and a station of honor in society.

But while religion is accorded honor in society, it is also severely excluded from participation in public life. Like the drum major we have the honor of walking ahead, but nobody expects us to play in the game. Because of our rules about freedom of religion, we are thought to belong to a separate league.

The battle for students' souls today is often won by those systems of thought — those philosophies — that are not strictly religious in our sense of the word. For these are free from legal restrictions and the emotional hang-ups that keep some from believing. These world views may be taught freely almost anywhere.

This fact produces some ironic paradoxes. We may talk in the classroom about Karl Marx, but not about Jesus Christ. We may examine the design of creation provided we do not mention the Designer. We may enact a rain dance, but we may not pray. If a man advocates personal degradation and calls for the downfall of our society, we might well welcome him to speak on campus. But if the speaker is quote the Bible freely, he is probably too sectarian to be admitted.

If in a classroom of thirty students, twenty-nine of them believe in God and would wish some form of devotional exercise, their wishes can be vetoed by the one remaining student if his parents complain. Why can one overrule the twenty-nine? Because atheism is not a religion. In other words, our belief that the universe is personal cannot be allowed to compete with the atheist's belief that the universe is impersonal, because unbelief is welcomed anywhere but belief is not.

If the church and its educators are to escape from such unfair restrictions, we must rethink and enlarge our understanding of what religion is. It may be that in narrowing the term to a suitable exclusiveness we have fashioned our own trap.

The Old Testament's treatment of idolatry may provide a clue as to where we should begin. Whatever kind of image a man bowed to, that was his god.

Whatever possessed his soul, that was his religion. Whatever he trusted in was what he thought to be his savior. Whatever triumphal ending he hoped for; that was his idea of heaven.

But consistently these unworthy idolatries were considered to be religions. Translated into today's terms, Americans are idolatrous too. And when they are seen as such, the very rules of our contest for the minds of the students will change. Then it will be clear that we have kept out of our schools only the official religion, allowing some unofficial religions to be practiced there.

In fact, if we broaden our definition, we can assert that there is a strong religion in many public schools now. It is humanism, the belief that man himself is supreme, that he can solve his own problems, and that he is even responsible for his own origins. Moreover this humanism is often monopolistic and intolerant; in the name of peace and objectivity it silences opposing views. Even talk of right and wrong, of good and bad, are considered inappropriate because they infer an ultimate standard.

It will be a long and difficult task to broaden the public's concept of what religion is. But it is the only way out of the grossly unfair set-up we have now. Under the present system, we have removed ourselves from effective witness in the public schools. But as a worthy religion among many unworthy idolatries, we can have a fair chance to be heard.

This is not to discount the persistent efforts of devout teachers whose personal faith radiates light into the classroom. Their personal witness is to be commended and encouraged. But we must attack the injustices of the present system also. Too long traditional Christianity has guarded its exclusive honors without realizing that it now has the honor of being excluded. ❧

Chapter 3:
The Church in a
Secular Society

This chapter explores the intersection of a Christian world view with a secular society that is less and less tolerant of that view.

The Foreigner

1943. *Written around the time Lincoln began preaching in his first church in Manchester, New Hampshire.*

A stranger came to our church one night
He sat in a pew alone;
And as he listened, his eyes grew bright
With light from the Father's throne.

After the hush of the closing prayer,
A friendly murmur began;
And we shook hands with the stranger there
As only our people can.

We chatted a bit with him, to show
We were his friends indeed;
And we asked him what we wanted to know —
This question: "Are you a Swede?"

"You're not a Swede?" — somewhat surprised,
"I see, you just dropped in;
Well, whenever you're passing by
You're welcome to stop in."

"He's not a Swede," the whisper came
With disappointed frown;
So then we did not ask his name
Or if he lived in town.

The stranger has not come again —
I sometimes wonder why;
Although he wasn't one of us
He might as least stop by.

❧

Judgment

June 1, 1971. *This article originally appeared in the The Covenant Companion.*

"It's not for me," my neighbor said,
"Religion I don't dig. Like judgment, sin,
And all that jazz." He smiled a little
Condescendingly, and turning, walked away.
I stood there, watched him go.
I cried within myself, "Lord, I believe,
Help thou my unbelief and answer me,
Is there still a judgment day?"
Now night arrives. I try to rest,
But sleep eludes me. And to my brooding mind
A distant vision soon appears,
I see with inward eye how judgment comes —
No trumpets. Just the inevitable march of time
Bringing us its punishments and its rewards,
The cause that culminates in its effects,
The journey that must end in destination,
The widening of life's great river
As we delay our crossing to the Kingdom,
The somber reaping where our hearts have sown.
All these are judgment. Even nature
Tells us of a cosmic wrath to come —
The graying of the skies around us,
The dying of life-giving streams,
The creatures of the forest gone,
The concrete ribbon slashing through the meadow,
The people crowding, standing in each other's way.
When leaders that we chose betray our trust,
When criminals conspire to bleed the poor,
And no one cares enough to rescue them,
When we demand our rights convincingly,
Shunning our responsibilities,
Giving less, demanding more, in flagrant mockeries

Of work that claim the task well done —
Is this not judgment?
A dismal reaping what our hearts have sown?
Since I have seen the judgment process
So inexorable, so personal, so intimate in its discerning,
So fitted to the kind or callous deed,
So patient in its long delay, I know, I know
That God is there. Beyond the limits
Of my finite mind, I can discern
As light must wane at ending day
That in the onward process is a patient voice,
Beyond foreboding skies a loving, grieving Father.
I know in faith that judgment emanates from him.
There comes indeed a day when sheep and goats are parted,
The blessed and the cursed. And I believe.
At last my troubled heart is quieted. God rules,
This is his kingdom still. And I can sleep.
❧

Is All Charity Christian?

January 15, 1976. *This article originally appeared in The Covenant Companion.*

The editor of our local newspaper writes an editorial about the danger of bei a Good Samaritan. Fire destroyed the house where a mother with several you children lived, leaving them destitute. The editor issued an appeal for funds the family. Money came in, and a checking account for a generous amount was up at the nearby bank. In a short time the editor was notified that the account v overdrawn, and that it was his responsibility to correct the situation. Apparen the mother had written checks well in excess of the amount in the account, a then had left town with her brood.

We all know of instances in which the good deed was not rewarded b scorned-or the giver even abused or endangered. The witness to the crime who detained longer than the accused and is threatened; the last-minute volunteer a church supper who gets left alone to clean up; the motorist who is robbed the hitchhiker he has picked up; the firemen who are shot at as they answer t false alarm; the cheerful giver who finds that most of her money never reaches announced destination.

Outcomes like these are dismaying and baffling to the Christian. How c people return evil for good? How can the cup of cold water be thrown back in the face of the giver? Must so much of our seed fall among thorns? As God liv should not the reward be inherent in the act itself? Can the good tree bring foi such evil fruit?

Some of the teachings of Jesus are held in high regard in our country, particula those that have to do with physical well-being. When catastrophe strikes, summon resources and make loans available. We spend a high proportion of o taxes to educate our children. Through federal programs and pensions we try make life easier for the poor and the aged. And organizations established for go causes flood our mailboxes with literature imploring us to give.

But we are getting cynical about such programs. The benefits we offer to soi become a heavy burden for others, and the bureaucracy handles the money wastefully. We hear so much about fraud and theft in medical programs th we are horrified. In short, too much of our supposed benevolence — willing unwilling — goes down the drain or into the pockets of charlatans. Are we still believe that "the greatest of these is [charity] love"? (*1 Corinthians 13:13*) Are these large scale attempts at Christian mercy futile? The evil in human nature seems to crush them down.

In fact, Christian presuppositions are sometimes used as weapons against those who profess his name. Why do children often walk in the middle of the road, not allowing motorists to pass? Their reasoning must be that since adults are supposed to consider the welfare of children uppermost, they would not dare to ask for the right of way. I have heard that people on welfare have in some places formed unions to demand more of what society gives them. Or try these hypothetical quotations:

"Since as a Christian you should love your neighbor, you will say nothing while I trample your flowers."

Or, "Since society has granted me security in my job, I will take advantage by doing less and less work."

Or, "Since society has granted me freedom on bail before my trial, I will take advantage of that leniency by committing another crime."

We have difficulty making Christian charity operative because we have forgotten a basic fact: Christian charity requires the presence of Christ. The teachings of Jesus were not intended to operate without the Teacher. The fruit does not appear except from the tree. The ethic is powerless without its reason for being. As the resolve needs its dynamic, and the good intent needs a driving compulsion, so the good advice of the New Testament moves into life only under his auspices. "...Just as the branch cannot bear fruit by itself unless it abides in the vine, neither can you unless you abide in me," (*John 15:4*) says our Lord.

The effect of the charity and the meaning of the deed still depend on the persons involved, and on their motives. Two young men are interested in the same girl. One is welcome, the other is not. A gift is delivered to her house. Never mind what the gift is; if it's from Christopher, it's beautiful; if it's from Homer, ugh. The who is more than the what. A gift from a loving parent may have some hidden strings: we trust you are behaving yourself while we provide for you in this way. The love in the gift produces some kind of pressure in the recipient to conform. In fact, love always does that. Love is a force acting upon the one loved.

If we compare a government handout with a gift in the name of Jesus, we can see some startling differences. One is impersonal, the other is personal. One is in response to a specific need; the other is an attempt to set a certain standard of living. One is temporary with a more permanent effect; the other is permanent with a temporary effect. Compare the missionary's use of the dollar with the inefficiency of a government agency.

The Christian's assessment of a situation is a part of the wisdom of God. He can see whether his efforts are bearing fruit. There is an unspoken, implicit "Go your way, and from now on do not sin again" (*John 8:11*) involved, which is what makes the work of the Christian agency effective.

In fact, true charity may not lie in the gift or the good turn at all, but in God himself and in the love these activities express. The New Testament hints at this. The alabaster box of ointment poured out was more effective, according to Jesus, than giving something of equal value to the poor, as Judas suggested.

The thrust of a Christian concern is not the same as that of a strictly humanitarian agency. When Jesus fed the multitude, this was a secondary task; the real answer to their need lay in this message. Christ does not espouse a certain standard of living; he requires a response of responsibility. He does not speak of rights without corresponding duties. He does not respond to the demands of the unthankful. He does not teach that one can by possessions alone insulate himself from the dark moments of the future. The wisdom of Jesus Christ keeps his followers from being entrapped by a generation that so badly misunderstands the essentials of life.

The godless charity, dealing more with symptoms than with causes, is usually helpless before the real problem, which is human sin. Money will not cure it, though the world may think so. Greed, envy, a self-centered view of life, deceit, laziness, pride, and a thousand types of theft are things that make our programs futile, and only Jesus can speak to these. The "Great Society" falls flat because it cannot handle the corruptions of human nature. "...Apart from me you can do nothing" (*John 15:5*) is an oft-demonstrated truth here.

It is a shame that the churches have so completely turned over the work of the Good Samaritan to public and government agencies. For the very genius of the gift is love, and the genesis of that love is God as revealed in Jesus Christ.

Unfortunately much of the government's giving is not giving at all; it is taking from the unwilling taxpayer, giving to a group that can deliver the desired votes nd passing on a large part of the debt to our children. Church people seem ometimes to be confused as to the difference between Robin Hood and Jesus. imply transferring possessions from one to another is not necessarily God's ntention.

Unless His life is involved, no blessings flow. Unless a Christian spirit prevails, ne gift is bare; it needs the Great Giver. Government billions cannot change notives, but Jesus can. If we follow only because we ate of the loaves and rere filled, we will be disappointed. The life abundant cannot be reckoned in ollars. ❧

Jesus Saves Two Ways

2002. *Originally published on the Internet.*

Jesus saves in two ways. The one that evangelicals declare is that by paying the price for our sin Jesus allows us to enter His kingdom. When that happens, the Holy Spirit enters our consciousness. A different kind of awareness — a feeling that we are forgiven and that God lives within us appears. We are saved. If our acceptance is total, our redemption is total also. Many a church survives for years on the memory of that experience.

But I insist that Jesus saves another way also. Jesus saves society and community and civilization. For wherever belief in Christ appears, characters are changed for the better. When these changed people act out their beliefs they begin to affect life around them.

In one sense this is not a different kind of salvation; it is simply the living out of the first kind. In fact the second kind exists only when it is grounded in the first; its basis is conversion, the new birth, the changed heart. But because we have only identified the first, let us call this working out, this identification with the group as well as the individual a second way Jesus saves.

This second sense has a factor going for it that the first does not: it persists dying very slowly. A rejection of God's love causes the door to close immediately but the effect of Jesus in society dies very slowly, and can be renewed many times In our own country many of the customs that Jesus caused are still with us in spite of the tirade against Christ in the last fifty years.

This influence can be felt by those who claim they are atheists and scoffers. They may respect the traffic signal not because of any willingness to observe the commandments; the signal is a good idea. The dim awareness that other people are as good as we and have rights which we must respect may not appear on the surface, but it was God's idea in the first place. Improvements in society are based on the source of all good. Human nature does not yield to respect for others without the basic cause being God, the source of all good.

This influence begins in the holiness of a few; martyrs die until somehow they become the seed of the good change. More people are touched by their example a movement takes place, and it may even become law. Whether it gets that strong not, it goes to celebration and custom, and custom gets entrenched for a long me. Those who never hear about Jesus are nevertheless affected. For a teaching keep its effect requires much holy living; the kingdom persists as long as its bjects obey plus the permanence of law and custom.

Our attempts to make the saving of the soul the whole work of Jesus causes us set aside some of the Gospel story as grand, but irrelevant. Perhaps laudable, t not a part of Jesus' main purpose. Jesus stills the storm; wonderful, but not sential to God's main purpose. The miraculous draught of fishes: wonderful, but ill beside the point. So we begin to restrict God's greatness to Christ dying for r sins, and the rest is window dressing.

But these "non-salvation" instances are a part of the second way Jesus saves. He eds the five thousand. It is both a demonstration and a beginning of the way the fluence of Jesus feeds people. Our organizations organized to feed the poor and provide for the needy are based on Jesus' love and receive their impetus from the ve of God. He cures the demoniac; In Jesus' name we organize to counsel and help those whose minds fail them.

Via the Good Samaritan and his merciful help most of our medical system ists and lengthen and improves life. Not just an idea from our Lord; no, the real ower to rise above our faulty human nature and act comes from Jesus, who in this ay is saving the world.

I know not of any similar force that makes the community better. The whole anoply of God's qualities are available to the believers.

Dare I say that fifty percent of salvation has not even been recognized? Unless e recognize the external half, we shall lose the inner, the individual part also. ❧

Jesus - Savior of Society

1998. *Originally published on the Internet.*

In the past forty years Christianity has been dealt a serious setback. From bein highly respected in these United States, we have fallen into near disgrace. On we were expelled from public schools, the idea that religion should be separate from public life got increasing velocity, until a virtual witch-hunt ensued. Schoc principals were on the watch for any sign of that forbidden piety.

The witch-hunt has abated, but the no-God rules are still in force. Highe education expresses its disdain and warns incoming students to leave their piet at the door.

It is clear that we, who are many, must learn how to speak collectively to fulfi our mandate to bring Christ to our nation. But how? I cannot claim to have an answers.

For the past three years it has been dawning on me slowly that as far as I ai concerned, I am assigned to a tiny part of this task. I have no explanation why th should have become my obsession. At the farthest stretch of my imagination, might say that God wants me for this, but I dare not claim that much connectio with the Lord. That the Lord could use someone this old is quite unlikely.

At any rate, the vision has been clearing slowly to where I can begin to expre: it. I am embarrassed by the long years of ministry in which it did not dawn on m the word "politics" was always said with disgust or derision, and I bought that.

I do not hope to weaken the soul's salvation by looking at society; the corporat must have the personal as its foundation. If anything I say makes sense, it shoul be that the individual's involvement must not be lessened; "Jesus saves" is primar Involving the group, the nation, is simply a further step in claiming Jesus a Lord.

If you are with me thus far, we had better start looking at ways to carry ou this neglected commission. As our failure covered at least a generation, so w must expect that any kind of recovery will take that long. We have loved foreig missions as long as they were far enough away so that responsibility did not touc us; and we still like Sudan, the depths of Africa, and the interior of China. But a the world shrinks, we must deal with places close enough to cause responsibility.

1. **We must vote.** We will never tell which party or which cause; you must realize that from what you hear in church. In the near future, the Christians may organize their own party. Always, whatever glorifies God. We must render to Caesar what is due him, "Let every person be subject to the governing authorities." (*Romans 13:1*) To not vote is not a Christian option; as children of Hope, we must.

2. **Axioms.** Having indicated that we will take the battle out into the marketplace, we need to remind ourselves of the power of God to save in this marketplace. These thoughts worry me, because I have not heard them said exactly as I would say them; yet when I ask others about them, I hear agreement about them.

    a. All good comes from God. Wherever good appears on earth, the Spirit is God is the agent of change. This must include otherwise ungodly situations; if the choice is made for the benefit of a person or mankind, it is God who by His Spirit causes that choice another step toward his will.

    b. Humanity cannot rise above its present level by the force of its will; the only way to make a good change is to allow God to enter; His is the redeeming force. Just as individually we cannot make light, but we can go to where it is, and arrange for that light to shine on us.

    c. In His love, God is always pressing in on us, awaiting the permission of our wills; the Spirit will come in to us if we allow Him. If we believe in Jesus, that is our permission for God to enter.

    d. This permission may be made somewhat permanent by accepting customs that honor God, or by laws that bend people toward obedience. Sometimes a whole generation can enjoy the yoke that is easy, and the burden light, before the veneer of righteousness collapses.

    e. When and where the Spirit of God is resisted, the society that once welcomed it will begin to crumble. More laws and more enthusiasm will fail to preserve it. "Unless the Lord guards the city, the guard keeps watch in vain." (*Psalms 127:1*) There is ample evidence of this in our newspapers.

3.   **We need to admit that we are our brother's keeper, and act accordingly.** For example, in the days of the Roman Empire, there were devastating epidemics in 165 A.D. and beginning again in 251 A.D. About thirty per cent of the population was killed in each case. The response of the Christian church was quick and impressive; they willingly tended the sick — not only the Christian sick, but the heathen too. The general populace showed no sympathy; even the family would flee from the sick. Thousands died unattended. The Roman emperor complained that the official priests didn't care, but that the Christians did. The great and selfless mercy shown by the church did much to gain their final acceptance in the empire.

The command of Jesus in Matthew 25, the parable of the Good Samaritan, and the example of Jesus in the Gospels has left us with no choice; we must serve.

In the Middle Ages the church served as hospital, as medical help to a world that had little sympathy for the dying. The mercy of Christ continued thru the centuries; what little know-how they had they used; their greatest contribution was that they loved as Jesus loved.

When love leads the way - that is - when the acts of mercy precede the items of belief, doors will open. It is when our doctrine is louder than our love that society resists the changes that Christianity will cause. ❧

Thoughts on the Separation of Church and State

April 1, 1983. *This article originally appeared in The Covenant Companion.*

In recent years, when evangelicals have achieved enough prominence to be noticed on the national scene, their early successes have been followed by numerous setbacks. Partly through the efforts of the ACLU and other watchdog organizations, rulings have been made by the courts which curtail or deny previously held privileges. Moreover, in situations where Christianity had long been influential beyond its doors in public life, it seems that decisions have been almost uniformly against the right of the church to be there.

One phrase has been particularly damaging: separation of church and state. That phrase is taken to be a condensation of the proper role of religion as defined in the First Amendment. But its meaning is almost the reverse; whereas the First Amendment seeks to protect religion from the inroads of government, this phrase is used to bar religion from government and, by implication, from those it governs. At almost every juncture where the question has arisen, it has served to separate the church a little further from public life and utterance.

Anguished cries have been heard from those who would oppose church and para-church organizations on this matter. "They are interfering!" "They are trying to force us into their religion!" Apparently such people forget that every individual and every pressure group has an equal right to make itself heard and to influence government.

So wherever the question has been raised, "Does religion belong here?" the answer has been, "No, because of the separation of church and state."

So far, efforts to slow this trend have been inadequate. I am convinced that the verdict does not lie in arguments over particular situations; it lies in the assumed rules of the game-in assumptions made before the arguments begin.

These assumptions seem to be:

1. That life without religion is the normal state.

2. That religion is an addition, a frosting which may make life more bearable or enjoyable.

3.   That religion should not be allowed to invade the privacy or challenge the thinking of those who choose not to indulge in it.

The church must recognize these unspoken ground rules for what they are, false premises. It must also challenge them, by assertions such as the following:

Regarding assumption No. 1: Religion is innate in all human beings. In the same way that temperature is basic to all matter, so every individual assesses values as worthy or unworthy, and seeks the highest of these chosen values. That for most people these are not a part of an organized system of thought does not make them less real. In other words, the name religious could be applied to our common idolatries.

Regarding assumption No. 2. Everyone chooses some highest good to venerate: wealth, health, leisure, acceptance, fame, status, intelligence, and many others.

Regarding assumption No. 3. The issue is not between religion and no religion, but over what values best serve humankind. It is true that so many travesties have been perpetrated in Christ's name that the reputation of the Church is far from unsullied. Yet it is generally conceded — even though grudgingly — that no higher standard exists; that whenever you try to define a supreme good, you define Christ. Whatever values a nation desires for its citizens tend to be those espoused by the Gospel.

Our kind of government places great reliance on the good character of it citizens to carry out the responsibilities of office and citizenship. In fact, ou government breaks down to the extent that its people do not have the qualitie which are taught by Christianity. It follows then that a Christian presence an influence are essential, yes, critical to the survival of representative government.

So it is doubly ironic that we are forced to play with this stacked deck, to argu facing false premises. I am convinced that unless we make great efforts to chang the rules, we shall continue to lose the argument. Here are three suggestions as t how that might possibly be done:

1.   We must yield up our insistence that we are unique. At present we clai a favored position, yet have less right to be heard. If we argue that on organized religion is entitled to representation or existence, we appear

unbelievers as a tenant who shows signs of claiming ownership, as a group claiming right not by acceptance but by some claimed precedence. We cannot continue to press for recognition because we are "religion;" that only makes things worse.

2.   We must consider broadening our definition of religion to include the common forms of idolatry, to some extent like the Old Testament definition. This would involve a continuing effort to point out to the public that such idolatries are forms of religion also. It would be a long process. But it would make Christianity one of many, not the one and only, and from that position we would be able to press for our right to be heard. While we claim a monolithic divine right, we have been adjudged that we do not belong. But as a point of view among other points of view, we can be back on the field of play again.

3.   Now we can begin to plead equality of opportunity. "If I believe that there is Someone up there, and you don't, why is my view suppressed, and yours is not?" "If you may teach freely in public schools about Karl Marx, why may I not teach about Jesus Christ?" "If you think the universe came about by blind chance, and I think it was designed by a Supreme Intelligence, why is the teaching of my view forbidden, and yours acceptable?"

To us, Christianity is much more than a point of view, but we must argue at this level to avoid its increasing exclusion, and gain at least equal access for our beliefs. So long we have prided ourselves on being the leader of the school band, only to discover that we are not welcome at the game where the real decisions are made.

This path is not without cost. If we plead that we ought to have as much right anyone else, it follows that we shall have no more right than anyone else. But would open the way for a more effective witness. As one of many, at least our national faith in fair play would be on our side. ❧

Hardly Soul-Winning

1998. *Originally published on the Internet.*

Once upon a time, it was expected of every believer that they attempt to b a soul-winner; that is, to persuade someone to become a Christian. When th U.S.A. had considerable influence in society, even the scoffers were not too fa from the kingdom of God, and the question of commitment was not far away.

In the last fifty years, however, the spiritual status of the average citizen has n only been reduced to nothing, but the citizen, influenced by a heathen media, ha become a foe of the faith.

Thus our chance of bridging the gap by conversation and friendship is nil. is still our commission that we make disciples of all nations, but the task is no much more difficult. If in the past we believers thought that our task was to brin someone up on a mythical scale of "goodness" from a reasonably good score of "6 to a perfect score of "10" on a scale of 1 to 10, now we find that the unbeliever we are trying to reach are not at "6"; they are at zero or one.

Complicating the situation is the fact that churches still think that the task to bring unbelievers from their "goodness" score of 6 to perfection at 10, leavin a chasm of soul-winning inactivity on that scale between "1" and "6." The gulf evident in Christian radio programs: Unless one uses the sacred terms exclusive — one must sound like a sermon — the churches will not fund such a program We cannot bear to realize that the gulf between believers and unbelievers can b that vast.

I believe that God has shaped my life and experience so that with His help I ca be effective in reaching the scoffer. I did not ask for this assignment, and I consid myself unworthy of even trying. But the burr is under the saddle, so I have n choice but to be willing and look for opportunities to express myself in that caus I readily admit the foolishness of attempting something new at my old age; if m health closes down soon, I am content. But that God has pointed at me for som task the implications of which I am still unaware, that conviction I cannot shak

What I write, therefore, and what I will say if given a chance, is whatever seem to me to be the next logical step toward the kingdom. Because this approach designed to reach the unbelievers we would identify as operating between zero an one, the approach may not seem like the usual evangelism to those accustomed to the vocabulary of the church. But my choice of words are inseparable from my calling; I must reach the unbelievers where they are.

Here are my thoughts as to how we shall approach those who do not believe in Jesus Christ. The approach is not direct, unless we recognize that the other person is in obvious crisis. For the most part, we are companions on the road, but our conversation contains an emphasis on the kingdom as we see it. We do not confront; we travel as companions. What we are in Christ will become evident.

1. **Talk about the Creation**. Almost all science, botany, physiology, astronomy, and biology are the subject matter. It ranges from being glad it's a nice day to some new fact we have lately found, like the bean sprout that knows which way is down, and can't be deceived. The weather is good, whatever it is. All of this brings us to a Creator who designs the flower and the snowflake, who is utterly dependable. The design presupposes a Designer; what other source is there for beauty? It shows a greater mind than ours which can handle complexity far beyond our understanding - the way molecules are put together to form different elements. The Maker of all this is intelligent; He can know not only botany but human minds as well. Design, Complexity, and Intelligence; no one has it to that extent but God; we rest in that Great Mind.

2. **Talk about wrongdoing**. The tragic waves of crime that sweep over us will certainly enter our conversation at some point. Is it because we don't know any better? Are the people so unschooled that they don't know how to act? What code of behavior do we need? There is a right way to live; it has been proven right and necessary by two thousand years of history. When we turn to God, He will guide our next move, and when He is involved in the decisions made in our community, they will be the right decisions. If the subject at hand is about someone close to us, there is a greater need to know what is right. Our confidence in the Gospel at this point will be important. Also important is that we admit our own failings; we are fellow sinners who need God.

3. **Talk about uncertainty**. This an easier one — the fragileness of life, the fact that we are driven along by time, and that we do not know what tomorrow brings. The crux of our thinking is this: what happens after death? Our attitude shall be one of quiet certainty that through Christ we

47

shall live again. When the loved one of our friend dies, we cannot promise eternal life for that person, but we can reiterate the terms by which we are accepted. The invitation of Jesus to life to come is always open; the acceptance of that invitation on one's deathbed does not disqualify it. Offering this invitation is a tremendous gift that is ours to give. It may be tempting to use church vocabulary, but be careful; religious jargon turns people off. The idea can be stated in everyday language better. The love shown by faithfully visiting the unbeliever, by just spending time with them is a good persuader, provided that the effort is genuine.

4. **Talk about imprefection**. Another of the method of getting people to think about God is to discuss original sin. That failing is in each of us; no matter how high-minded and devout we are, we will still come up with something imperfect, and given enough rope, we will hang ourselves with it. The citizenry in general does not think in these terms, and does not believe that they are essentially imperfect. The need to defend oneself as to both veracity and purpose blinds us. Everybody else may be wrong, but we are not. The government is stupid, but I am not. The school systems are foolish, but I am not. It is this very self-importance that is our downfall, and at the point of our downfall the spirit of God has its chance. Here the Christian reminds the friend that we are all like that, and that God loves us anyway; that it is this fatal flaw that caused God to send His Son. The crush of the ego is the opportunity for the love of God to come in. If it is someone close by who has acted foolishly, condemnation is not appropriate; forgiveness is. If it is government that has dashed our hopes we are still its citizens, and we will add our integrity, such as it is, to the situation. It is never a me-versus-you situation; as believers, we are a part of the imperfection, and we admit it.

5. **Talk about interdependence**. Another avenue into the heart of the sufferer is the individual-versus-group syndrome. We in these United States have been fed independence without measure and without thought of consequence. Our family ties have been weakened in the name of independence. Commitment becomes a dirty word; church membership becomes an afterthought to the believer. There is a place for independence but not in the spiritual life. If by the grace of God we learn to serve others we will find that that service is returned; in our difficult times there is a large and loving family to help us.

So to bring someone closer to the kingdom of God, bring them in by offering companionship and love as it exists within the fellowship of the church. Bear your heart, bear witness to Christ's salvation, and love as He first loved us. ❧

The Source of Character

2000. *Originally published on the Internet.*

We all know that America is sinking morally; that there is a level of honest and integrity that is going down. The companies we trusted we can trust n longer; even those with the greatest responsibilites seem not to uphold them. Th banks, the citadels of education, the professional sports, the supposedly successfu churches, the many arms of government, the people whom we trusted because w have known them so long, the artists, and the scientists all have become afflicte with this moral weakness, and what was wrong and unthinkable is now acceptab and even commonplace. What went wrong?

That the downfall seems to affect everybody is a sure sign that it had to do wit that which is common to all of us, our soul. This diagnosis assumes that our fait does produce character, that there is something within it that does improve it. An religion professes good, that we are encouraged to be good. It assumes that th more seriously you are religious, the better person you will be. True, but that only saying that you will get out of it what you put into it. Any human effort ha its reward; exercise and lift weights and you will be strong; run long distances an you will be better able to do so - simple cause and effect.

If the Buddhist tells me that he is a better person because of Buddha, I believ him. Human effort produces human betterment. The Old Testament sounds lik this; obey the Lord, and He will bless. Keep Israel faithful to Jehovah, and He wi give you peace and good crops. The history of Israel is proof that this is true.

But belief in Jesus Christ is a different matter. He does not primarily say "Do He says "Believe." You don't get out of Christianity what you put in; you get muc more. This is not human effort multiplied; this is a force outside of nature, outsid of humanity; this is a divine force that you cannot earn, yet it is given freely. It not our striving; it is God giving. Christ has a power that changes character for th better, and he is the only force that can do so.

How shall the Christ and that character be received?

1. You must believe that Jesus is now alive and has all the powers he showe during his time on earth. Without that certainty, the Son of God becom too subjective, a reflection of our own thinking.

2. You must accept that God in Jesus knows our thoughts and motives. It is not a philosophical matter; we cannot describe without realizing that the earnestness, the love of God is not just an aspect, a description. Just as you would deal with the sun, the heat and the light are so much the sun that other qualities are secondary, so in thinking of God, you must feel that he searches within you, "it is able to judge the thoughts and intentions of the heart." (*Hebrews 4:12*)

3. So Christ as God has arrived at your heart, to make some change there. Everywhere in Scripture we read of the longing of God to restore humankind to their original condition, that of perfect sinlessness. We cannot even visualize a conversation between mortal and God without this being the only agenda. Darkness cannot stand close to light without being affected; so nearness to God - that searching ache within - is ready to come in; in fact, He knocks at the door.

4. All that is left now is permission to enter. God gave us free will, and he will not enter unless we say yes. But this is horribly difficult; we like to be our own god, and do what we please. The whole history of humanity hangs on this decision. If we can say "yes," then Christ comes in with all His cleansing power. Insofar as we experience Him, we have a change in character. "Here is the Lamb of God who takes away the sin of the world!" (*John 1:29*) ❧

Part II:
Church Life

Chapter 4:
The Business of the Church

This chapter's essays discuss issues and offers answers for imperfect believers who struggle to live out their faith in front of each other, inside the church walls.

The Ransomed and the Obstinate

November 1, 1975. *This article originally appeared in The Covenant Companion.*

The Reformation restored to us a great truth: we have direct access to God. No intermediary is needed. Every believer is a priest, privileged to "approach the throne of grace with boldness." (*Hebrews 4:16*)

As evangelicals we have become the willing heirs of the emphasis. Since we define Christianity primarily as a relationship with God, we argue that coming into his presence is the very act that brings life and power to mankind.

Since those around us know that we insist on this communication, they have a right to expect that we do what we defend and profess. The results of that meeting at the mercy-seat should be clearly evident. We know what qualities ought to appear in the human heart after a meeting with the Almighty. Let us ask ourselves now whether these qualities do appear in our lives and in the lives of others who call themselves evangelicals.

Obviously reverence is such a quality. Who can "see God" and not be changed? A brilliant sunset can fill us with awe, and a starlit sky can shake us with its vastness. But these scenes are only small, impersonal specks in creation. If we know that the Infinite One himself knows and loves us, how should we respond? An adequate answer would be beyond us.

Our sense of awe and wonder ought to be at least that strong in our services of worship. How much of the vastness and eternalness of God is amongst us? It is a troubling paradox that some who claim God most loudly as their own are least aware of His holiness and majesty.

The attempt in this last decade to make God approachable by being folksy has produced a regrettable amount of flippant attitudes, crude humor, sarcasm, and smart remarks — all as part of a service of worship. Is it possible to know him and yet join in such parody?

Another quality which should appear from our encounter with the Lord is humility. In his presence we realize our sinfulness, our finiteness, and our mortality. "Woe is me...my eyes have seen the King, the Lord of hosts" (*Isaiah 6: 5*) is the appropriate response, as it was for Isaiah.

But it seems to me that some of the most egotistical claims of authority have come from those who insist that since God is all-wise, their interpretation of Him makes them wiser than their fellow man. Since God commands, and since they represent God, obedience to their directives is the only way to glory.

This misconception is a frequent and devastating one in evangelical ranks. Failing to distinguish between creature and Creator, some leaders have placed themselves on pedestals. Their boundless self-confidence becomes a basis of faith among those who follow them. A thinly-veiled boasting, frosted liberally with references to the glory of God, has been the method by which they have led the uncritical.

Because as evangelicals we tend to rely more on personalities than on institutions, we are particularly easy prey for those who would build financial empires in Jesus' name. Here the Word of God must be our stability; our thoughts must be of him who "...did not regard equality with God as something to be exploited, but emptied himself..." (*Philippians 2:6-7*)

It takes much grace to have certainty in one's faith, and still not be smug. It takes much love to see sin everywhere without making one's self a judge. It takes God-given humility to declare his strength and our own weakness in the same breath, and do it sincerely. The temptation to hint that somehow we deserve to be saved is always with us. It is so easy to confuse being "glad that we are saved" with being the Pharisee who was glad "...that I am not like other people..." (*Luke 18: 11*). C.S. Lewis, in his book *Mere Christianity*, says this: "Whenever we find that our religious life is making us feel that we are good above all, that we are better than someone else — I think we may be sure that we are being acted on, not by God, but by the devil." [1]

Another area troubles me. From our cleansing experience with the Lord will come the feeling that his very name is holy. As the commandment puts it, "The Lord will not acquit anyone who misuses his name." (*Exodus 20:7*) I think that evangelicals as a group are careful about profanity. But that commandment means also that we must not use His name lightly. He is not to be the target of a joke that belittles his holiness or minimizes our lostness. We are not to name His name because someone is expecting us to use our religious vocabulary at that moment nor should we claim that the Lord guided us to do something in order to hide a baser motive. A complete inward honesty about or relationship to God is to be prized above a well-said religiosity.

Another thing about us is puzzling: We are commendably aware of the
ins of the flesh, but often seem insensitive about the "sins of the spirit." The
New Testament lists some of these as "enmities, strife, jealousy, anger, quarrels,
dissensions, factions..." (*Galatians 5:20*)

True, the sins of the flesh are more obvious and more easily proved. But an
attitude of prayer will certainly make us sensitive to wrong thoughts as well. "Test
me and know my thoughts." says the psalmist, "See if there is any wicked way
in me..." (*Psalms 139:23-24*). If God's Presence is cleansing, then little cleansing
must indicate less of his presence in our lives.

A business meeting of the congregation is an example of what I mean. It often
finds us at our lowest ebb spiritually. In trying to be as wise as serpents, we often
fail miserably to be as harmless as doves. Here these who are seemingly ransomed
often turn out to be distressingly obstinate.

Perhaps a recognizable part of our problem lies in the fact that our inward
commitments are so much more fragile and temporary than our outward
commitments. If our inward fire dies, are we going to admit that? Probably not.
After all, we have six months to go in our chairmanship of the group, or a year
on the board, or even two-and-a-half years more as a deacon. So we continue to
go through the motions; we must not suffer the acute embarrassment that would
come with telling the truth.

We who claim the presence of the Almighty God in our lives carry a tremendous
responsibility. Because so many people are watching, those who once followed the
gleam and then hardened their hearts can do great harm to the fellowship of which
they are still a part. ❧

The Annual Conference: An Allegory

Oct. 1, 1971. *This article originally appeared in The Covenant Companion.*

In the village called Complacency, far up in the highlands of the land of Serenity, the villagers met to choose one of their number to represent them at the annual conclave. This conclave had several fine purposes: it gave the people living in the scattered parts of the land a sense of brotherhood, it served as a focus for the solution of their national problems, and it united the inhabitants of the land in a common cause.

This year was particularly important, for news had spread through the land that all was not well beyond their borders. If this were true, the noble people of the village of Complacency would not hesitate to bring their compassion to the situation, to alleviate inequity and suffering among their most distant neighbors.

So they chose a man named Loyal to be their representative, and they invested him with authority to speak for them, and to engage in whatever commitment he would on their behalf. And Loyal, as he began his journey, felt himself to be the incarnation of their willingness to serve and the messenger of their lovingkindness.

Arriving at the conclave, Loyal was delighted at the friendliness with which he was received. He waited eagerly for the appointed time when he could carry the standard of his village into the vast hall where the pilgrims would assemble. For there would be brought into one great focus and one great force all the love and sympathy that brooded over the land of Serenity. There, certainly, good would conquer evil in one mighty stroke, and as the lightning releases the tension between earth and heaven, so the noble land would discharge its obligation toward its less fortunate neighbors.

When the great assembly began, Loyal was thrilled by the magnificent singing, the wisdom of the discourses, and the comradeship of fellow pilgrims. It was not until several days had passed that he realized that no great moment had taken place. Instead the discourses seemed to tell of a day to come when benevolence would radiate from every village so purely that very little national urging would be necessary. The climax, Loyal realized was not to be at the conclave, but among the citizens of each village. And then, too soon, the conclave was over.

As Loyal began the long trek back to his own village, it dawned on him that the great task for which he had traveled was still undone. The standard of the village which he had brought so proudly began to grow heavy in his arms. What he had envisioned as a dramatic act of sacrifice had turned into an unrelenting, dismaying duty.

When Loyal arrived at home, his friends gathered around him in a festive mood to welcome him. But Loyal spoke solemnly, aware of his great responsibility.

"I have come," he said, "to bring you news of a great task before us."

"We are glad you were so greatly impressed," replied his friends. "To hear you speak thus is heartening, for it means that your trip to the conclave was worthwhile."

"But the conclave was not an end in itself," protested Loyal. "It was a beginning."

"We are glad that the authority we entrusted to you has climaxed in all this fervor," they replied.

"But we must join together now in the great cause," Loyal pleaded.

"Your oratory is superb," applauded the citizens. "We are proud to have been a part of so noble a plan of action."

Loyal opened his mouth to speak again, but nothing came. And slowly, as the weeks went by, the fire of that great purpose died within him. ❧

Model of a Modern Evangelical

1965. *To the tune of "I am the Very Model of a Modern Major General" by Gilbert and Sullivan*

I am the very model of a modern evangelical,
I never sing a song that isn't wonderfully rhythmical,
I always wear this smiling face to show that I have faith, you see,
And add a Pious look whenever anyone is watching me.
For proudly do I wear my perfect nineteen-year attendance pin,
My witness to the fourteen classes I have now been teacher in;
Sometimes I am particularly blessed and filled with joy, as when
I get to sing in a quartet with lovely Mrs. Andersen!

Chorus: Sometimes I am particularly blessed ... etc.

I seldom read a book, for they are mostly filled with tales of sin,
Except the ones that Rev. Jones, our pastor must have studied in;
Instead we read King James, or better yet a modern paraphrase,
And soulfully deplored this younger generations evil ways!
We're generous to foreign missions if they're far enough from here;
We're moving to the suburbs for the immigrants are coming near;
To church I used to drive the kids that lived beyond the railroad track,
Until one Sunday morn they put a dent in my new Cadillac!

Chorus: To church I used to drive ... etc.

I'm really very loving to the people I can hardly stand,
I pass out tracts, and books of Acts, explaining till they understand;
I'm very much for law and order, fighting all things criminal,
Except for things like traffic tickets, where the fine is minimal.
I wave the flag, and watch parades, and sing God Bless America,
I'd rather be unpopular than join in some hysteria;
I often write my Congressman, and sometimes pray for presidents
To rescue me from neighbors, and from all ungodly residents.

Chorus: I often write my Congressman ... etc.

My bumper sticker clearly shows my reverential piety,
A pinnacle of virtue I, an emblem of sobriety;
And so in matters Biblical, political, and rhythmical,
I am the very model of a modern evangelical.

Chorus: And so in matters Biblical ... etc.
❧

To Kneel With One Leg

1996. *Originally published on the Internet.*

I see four mistakes in American Christendom. These errors constitute continuous situations, so that unless there is deliberate change, we continue on the wrong road.

The first is calling science the place of its ultimate trust, and so trying to fit the faith into what it sees in human knowledge. Many a clergyman has unwittingly explained to the parishioners that the primitiveness of Scripture and its harsh statements were due to the relative ignorance of the first and preceding centuries. The Bible means well, but we know better; we must round its sharp edges so that it speaks to our time.

Many a clergyman had become famous by this belittling; the corollary idea is that this eminent divine is more intelligent than the ancients could ever be, and therefore deserves a following. So pitiful as to be almost humorous, someone announces that his research proves that the New Testament was wrong, and of course he is right.

The result of all this is complete powerlessness; they are their own gods if they reserve the final judgment for themselves. You do not find these people in volunteer situations, or in the soup kitchens, or on the mission field. Numerous though they are, they can scarcely maintain their own congregations.

The second type of failure is related to the first; it is self-praise through the medium of tradition. The eastern seaboard, claiming over three hundred years, is a frequent locale for this. This item came over on the Mayflower; Bradford founded this church; the font is from Abraham's time; we repeat the vows used by early Puritans in Massachusetts; and Ralph Waldo Emerson spoke here a number of times.

All this, assuming it is true, is a veiled way of saying, "Aren't we wonderful? Such pride ruins any contact with God; this is not the mind that was in Christ Jesus. Or Jesus would remind them that, "they love to stand and pray...so that they may be seen by others. Truly I tell you, they have received their reward. (*Matthew 6:5*)

A third type of error in Christendom is reliance on the organization of which we are a part. Roman Catholics would be most prone to this. It is a comforting idea that someone else can take care of our soul for us, just as we hire someone to do for us what we cannot do. But Christ did not come to an organization. Neither did he make any guarantee that the groups which make up His church today would be the same ones tomorrow. Too much falling from grace is depicted in the New Testament itself to rely on organization over Spirit.

The final mistake of Christendom is involved in the hope of making our Faith popular. The complaint goes something like this: "The church should get with it! They are way behind the times. Everybody knows that sex is okay anytime." This position asks the church to forsake its message, which it cannot. Its message is the hope of the world. ❧

The Pilgrimage

2000. *Originally published on the Internet.*

I am fascinated to read about how other religions and even a combination of Catholicism and its observance when connected with local folkways can display a large variety of actions, parades, pilgrimages, handling objects, and calling these actions methods of worship.

I read how they handle sacred writings or just come near to them; how they dress to please God; how uttering cries and piercing their skins with designs is considered worthy; how they walk long distances to visit a place where something had happened long ago to make the spot holy. From our point of view, these things are foreign.

Because I am a Protestant who grew up in a time when only singing and praying and talking were permitted, I must ask, "Who's right?" Some practices so far from the beach of the Sea of Galilee I try to swallow, but cannot.

Yet I am in the minority; twenty centuries of this apparently meaningless worship, often to another God entirely, make so vast a witness that I cannot just call them wrong. I cannot believe that God ignored these people.

Our approaches to God, our ways of worship, are in some sense seen or heard by God. The pietist's attempts are also stumbling; God says I know what you mean by this, and credits it, if credit can be given. God reads the intention rather than the sleekness of the approach. The dancing around the golden calf in the wilderness may have been primitive, but the intent was clear. So God watches or listens, and He knows what we mean.

That admission makes much of the mumbo-jumbo admissible. When the person reaches out with his heart, I think there is a divine response, a feeling rising within the person that feels like some divinity. I kneel at the rock, and a little of the Spirit of God responds. There had to be something like that felt, or this would not have continued for all these centuries. They felt they were using their souls in the only way they understood.

That much credit I am willing to admit, but without the message there can be no meaning. I believe that the Holy Spirit is God himself; that when we allow Him into our meditations something of the character of God begins to change toward Him. But if you do not know of the gospel story, how can just a feeling change us?

Those denominations which emphasize worship, and correspondingly do not stress obedience to God, do poorly in making worthy citizens. The other extreme, just ethics without the need for salvation, is even worse.

My point is that God reads the intent of our worship and replies accordingly. But the pilgrimage on bleeding knees to the holy shrine does not sound like the Gospel. If only all that willingness could be used in the cause of redemption. ❧

My Message to the Church

2002. *Originally published on the Internet.*

My ministry is winding down. And so, in what seems to be this late hour, I fee that I must say it; this is my charge to the church.

Jesus came to this earth to save; not only to save the individual out of sin, bu also to save the world beyond the fact of saving the soul. For the saving of th individual is only the beginning; it is like Jesus saying to his disciples after H resurrection, "Peace be with you." (*Luke 24:36*) The three years of being wit the disciples had transformed them into leaders, now that they knew he ha conquered death. From that time the church began.

I think the church today has taken the half to mean the whole; to insist tha preparing individuals is the whole task. Then our Sundays are used to re-inspire th individuals. Just as the purpose and use of the automobile is not to keep its tan full, so neither is the church, as I see it, fulfilling its task by Sunday attendanc Preparation for the task is not the same as doing the task.

I praise the efforts that go beyond that; the missionaries that we support a great. But again, how much of that effort fills our love for Christ? The money tha goes to World Relief is very much on the mark, but it is not us; it is asking som few to do our work for us. Our support of the denomination is good, like buildir a place from which we could go out if we wished.

So my insistence is that we are doing half of what Jesus asked, and calling it th whole of the responsibility. That we are content with what we do only adds t the sadness of the situation. If a person just manages to stay alive, we give scar credit. And so for us.

We have church leaders who want to confine the message to the churc building, that anything outside is politics. That's bad; that's trying to limit th message to those who have already heard.

Believers in Christ could have a tremendous effect on our nation. The troub is partly that so many claim to be religious, but have no plans to participate. On would think that if we would like to have our nation be more affected by Chri we would at least vote, because legislators learn our wishes, and if our wish is tha Christ be honored, that will show. It is a shame that so few care.

If we cared, we could do something about all those people who cannot afford medical care, and so suffer. We would declare ourselves about obedience to the law, and Christ's law in us would be effective. We would keep pressure on the public school system, which by its refusal to honor God has brought up a generation that does not know even the decencies of living. We would send our children to Christian colleges, even if it means trusting God for getting the bill paid.

As a church, we must be continually at the task of helping those who need us, not only with money but what we could do by visiting them and filling in where they cannot at the present. The first three centuries of the Christian church were marvelous in their love for the heathens around them, caring for the sick even when the families forsook them. This is Christianity. If you love me, Jesus said, feed my sheep. This does not mean less worship; in fact, worship provides the strength to carry on for Him.

I know this will take a tremendous awakening. We have been inoculated by years of information without needing to act. Think of all those years of Sunday School without any urging to act on what we have heard. Dare I say that if you deal with the church only on Sunday, you learn to ignore the pleas; you can only take in so much.

There are many organizations which are based on Christian principles. Most try only a part, but do it well. They gather food, and they distribute it; they gather old clothes, and give them out. I hope they make clear that it is God's love that prompts them.

In recent years much effort has been made to limit the gospel, and it has been devastating. Do you even know about it? In this we must be willing to break the law and suffer the consequences. The next generation will be hostile to the church, and hostile to good laws. We have brought it on ourselves by refusing to care, and trouble is brewing. News of other countries where Christians are put in prison or even killed for their faith is a sign of what is coming unless we wake up and defend the right of the gospel to be heard. ✳

Chapter 5:
Church Membership

This chapter discusses church membership as the first step in becoming a part of the Body of Christ, and how taking that step brings unique responsibilities.

Consider the Body

November 15, 1976. This article originally appeared in The Covenant Companion.

The musicians in the orchestra had insisted on the dismissal of their conductor because of his obvious tyranny. Now they met to discuss their grievances with each other and to come to some understanding so they could function together. There was discrimination, there was bias, there was inequality, said some. It was not fair that a few had more chance to show off their virtuosity. Several complained that they had to play practically all the time while others rested for long intervals. Since some instruments were more expensive and some harder to transport, a way of taking that into account seemed necessary. Why not assign seats on a rotating basis, thus allowing every player the honor of being "first chair"? Or why not compensate the weaker-sounding instruments by giving them more solo parts. The flutists were critical toward the trumpeters for producing tones much too sharp and strident.

After several of these gripe sessions, compromises were reached and agreements were made, but no one was satisfied. A committee actually began revising a symphony to fit the new rules. But they soon realized that chaos would ensue, so they reported back to the group. Some still did not understand, however. How could so much fairness produce anything but good? Ought not democracy to issue in more beauty than tyranny? Would not unity of mind cause harmony of sound?

It is obvious to us that peace and unity so achieved is really only surrender to the petulance of individuals. Whenever the focus of an organization is no longer on its task, personal interests take over. Individual rights become the highest value rather than mutual responsibilities.

This is exactly what is happening to the people of the United States. Our traditional emphasis on individual freedom, coupled with the disdain of several and other important virtues, is becoming a destructive force. Yielding to one individual, one instance, or one pressure group at a time is more our style than acceptance of majority opinion or previous decision.

Heroes in America have always been individually perceived. The explorer, in spite of his crew, was considered a loner. The name of the patriot stood out above all others. The pioneer's vision was of what he could build all by himself. The

69

immigrant stood alone, and his family was his world. Though our governmen is vast and complex, we still tend to think of it in terms of one leader, whom w alternately trust or vilify.

Time Magazine referred recently to "the American idea of moving out, that a problems end with the horizon." For two centuries it was easier to move out tha to face our responsibilities where we were. And even though we ran out of frontie long ago, we still try to avoid being fenced in by the rights and needs of others. W would rather weaken the group and favor the individual. Crimes against societ (one hurting many) have been minimized. In fact, the idea that the "victimle: crime" is not serious seems to be gaining headway. Since the hurt and the cost ar spread among so many, who cares?

Ironically, this emphasis on the individual has its roots in the Christian gospe The one lost sheep, the lost son accepted on generous terms, knowing when th sparrow falls, the inclusion of little children-all these are evidence that in Chris the individual counts. But the parable assumes that the ninety and nine are safe i the fold, their security assured.

There was a time when English lords rode their horses across the farms of th peasants in pursuit of foxes. Today a well-financed pressure group can cut a simila swath through the welfare of the nation as a whole. Who defends the many again: the few? We don't know how. We keep setting aside the rules, "just this once."

It is the Bible that best teaches us a proper relation between the individual an the group. Members of a church are really members one of another, it says to u: and we do not belong to ourselves. Such statements we have commonly interprete in terms of our culture, with several grains of self. Doesn't the American believ that he is 90 percent independent and only 10 percent tied? No wonder ou allegiances are usually heavily discounted.

Actually, we were created to participate in a network of relationships: the famil the spouse, the friend, the neighbor, the relative, the people of God, the natior and the world. Most of our connections with these are thin. Some say that th reason for the current overemphasis on sex is that we lack the satisfactions othe relationships should supply.

Often organizations exist to glorify their leaders, to be a kind of pedestal on which the lauded general stands. Many have no inward unity but are held together by an outside restraint — like a bag of nails, looking single but actually full of sharp and irreducible elements.

How do you perceive your connection with others in the household of faith? Like teeth on a comb-with the same base, pursuing parallel courses? Like peas in a bowl — a lot of togetherness, not much friction, but no direction? Like spokes in a wheel-each heading in a separate direction, but with a central unity? Like threads in a cloth, where our differences make only strength and beauty and where our identities come together into one? The best metaphor is the Apostle's: we are to think of ourselves as members of each other, each dependent on the other, having a life together that we could not possibly have separately.

As believers in Christ, we must be alert to the difference between our intended role and those being proposed by our culture. "Doing your own thing" is far from Christian freedom. It is like watching a chipmunk raid our food supplies. He is so cute and he takes so little at a time that we haven't the heart to stop him until it is too late to save our supper. Just so, individuals and small groupings often weaken our society by distracting our attention from the whole.

We dare not allow this to happen much longer, for what we are in Christ is more than what we are as individuals. We need to hear and heed again our Lord's wise word to Peter: "Simon, Simon, listen! Satan has demanded to sift all of you like wheat, but I have prayed for you that your own faith may not fail; and you, when once you have turned back, strengthen your brothers." (*Luke 22:31-32*) ❧

71

You Must Say It!

2000. *Originally published on the Internet.*

The twentieth century in the United States was a time when the public influence of Christianity came in strong, was taken for granted, was challenged, faded, and then was swept down by a vigorous opposition that realized that defense for it had faded.

Those who rode it in the years of its supremacy, when it was taken for granted, have forgotten how to defend it. The outer symptoms of it, the Sunday worship and its kindred organizations, assumed that religion was as usual; it did not need to be questioned, or re-approved, or restated.

That was a mistake, for Christianity needs to be restated, redefined, and reexamined if it is to have continued vitality. It was not until its fuel, the Spirit was almost gone that we awakened to our serious lack of affirmatives.

Those who slept in the declining years seldom if ever had to affirm that they were a part of this commonplace religion. One could go to Sunday School for forty years and never need to declare one's commitment. The eggs were not candled to see whether they were genuine. Or in another metaphor, we saw that the water looked clear; we did not test it for purity.

Faith in Christ was not intended to be a hazy preference, because by it we trade one kingdom for another. It is crossing a crucial divide; it is changing our direction. So that change must be announced. Jesus said, "Everyone therefore who acknowledges me before others, I also will acknowledge before my Father in heaven." (*Matthew 10:32*)

Since God is concerned, we only need to say it once; we can be His forever. But we change; we have our highs and lows, and if we are hardly into the kingdom, we will experience ins and outs. So the affirmation of our choice cannot wait; it helps to make our vacillations into permanency.

So many years of silence on this count have even put us into embarrassment. "I took care of that years ago. It would be like renewing one's vows of marriage." The difference is that the Christ-vow is easily concealed. It is the declaration itself that reasserts its permanence.

Because we live in a society that assumes our basic selfishness, any silence on this count puts us in an awkward position. "Why didn't you tell us? Couldn't make up your mind?" The soldier in uniform is honored; the spy is never accepted.

True, much of the population simply says "I am basically a good person. I can count on a just and loving God accepting me." This is missing the point entirely; it is not our opinion that counts, just as the recruit cannot decide on what terms he will join the army. The "I am good" person has no reason to confess an allegiance to which he does not aspire.

I am of the belief that a church should ask for a confession of faith often. We will take heart and be strengthened thereby. Just as an army needs to parade often, both for itself and for the assembled crowd, so we need to raise the flag of faith, both for ourselves and for those around us. ⁂

The Dilemmas of Church Membership

May 1984 . *This article originally appeared in The Covenant Companion.*

What is church membership? It is an ungainly marriage of heaven and earth. I is the wind of the Spirit captured for duty. It is fire from the sky in an earthboun harness. It is wavering zeal confronted with an unrelenting task. It is infinit faithfulness circumscribed by a demanding schedule.

At its best, it is the key to the kingdom; at its worst, it is the stewardshi committee casting someone into the outer darkness. At its best, it is life's mos satisfying belonging; at its worst, it is a gradual hardening of the heart because o pride because one is a good person. At its best, it is the environment for etern: life; at its worst, it is deacons playing apostles without pity.

To make the inner light practicable, to guide the holy vow into Christia: charity, is a task which frustrates the leadership of many a church with its persisten dilemmas. Here are some of them.

If we apply literally the words and the example of Jesus regarding discipleshij we find very few who qualify. To take up one's cross and follow, to forsake house and brethren, to go the second mile, to turn the other cheek, to offer one's cloal to go out into all the world-these are qualifications which, taken literally, are no common among church members. It is apparent that in practice we have use more earthbound criteria to determine church membership. The vows made a the time of joining the church, though agreed to, are more apt to be considered a ideal toward which we strive than a requirement to be lived up to.

At the other end of the obedience scale, the dangers of leniency in determinin church vitality become readily apparent. It looks like an easy way to win th battle, but usually results in losing the war. The membership roll looks good an there may be an increase in attendance. But if spiritual life is not involved in th transaction, several unfortunate results will slowly become apparent:

1. There will be more dragging of feet in plans to do the Lord's will. A laggards in a parade slow the pace for all who follow, so the carn; members will choose self-indulgence over sacrifice and the self-interest o the organization over the spiritual obligations of the church.

2. When such members come into church office, their decisions will affect the long-term attitude of the church. To the extent that their influence is felt, it will be harder for the church to grow in grace.

Another persistent dilemma is found in the question of how much the leadership of the church can depend on observable phenomena in assaying another's membership — whether someone should be dropped, allowed to join, reprimanded, or exhorted. Who are we to judge another's relationship with God and their actions among people? We would rather not judge, lest we ourselves be judged, but if we are to have a realistic organization we must make responsible, even agonizing decisions.

Even the recitation of the vows cannot be considered the sole criterion for membership. These promises may seem like some of our patriotic utterances, high-minded in sound and skimpy in loyalty. On the other hand, to claim that no one really knows who is a Christian, and who ought to belong, is to put church membership on a basis entirely apart from the New Testament. Human judgment cannot be avoided.

If we set up a list of objective requirements for the prospective member, again human wisdom is not sufficient; the wind of the Spirit "...blows where it chooses, and you hear the sound of it, but you do not know where it comes from or where it goes." (*John 3:8*) The bedridden who cannot promise to attend, the destitute who cannot give adequately, those absent be cause they serve the Lord elsewhere, those who are afraid to speak up-they all run afoul of our rules, though God will welcome them.

Those churches who insist on a certain act or a specialized way or expressing one's faith as the only valid door to salvation only exacerbate this misunderstanding. To take up serpents, to greet with a holy kiss, to wash each others' feet, to build stone altars, to call only certain phrases efficacious, to designate one place as being holier than another — all these and more are efforts to make the Holy Spirit more predictable, and thus we unwittingly appoint ourselves as keepers of the gate. "Gimmick" religion — taking any part and calling it the whole — is often attractive to the unthinking, and calls its success proof of its validity.

Another false standard of judgment is to measure the emotion shown. Plausible enough at first, it penalizes the solemn and the moody. It can become a cult of feelings. The cries of joy over one's salvation become standardized. Our joy counts more than his praise. The effect becomes more important than the cause.

The legacy of a common heritage was an unduly strong factor in our membershi policies for many years. The "our kind of people" idea drew lines where the should have been none, amplified the importance of a familiar culture, and ofte mistook an earthly country for a heavenly one.

The conflicting pressures within the congregation to include and exclude hav caused some to espouse a two-stage membership, one for the active, one for th inactive. By this reasoning, the awkward need to cross out names is seldom face. The active are counted for purposes of financial responsibility, while the inactiv including those long gone, the temporarily petulant, and the noncontributor are added to the others for public image purposes. Such a double standard unworthy, a manipulation of the count for temporary advantage.

There are denominations who practice a policy much different from ours. T them it seems that membership does not necessarily involve a promised person surrender to the lordship of Jesus. It means only that one is interested. The parab of the wheat and the tares is quoted as a basis for this practice. Assuming that w do not know who are the wheat and who are the tares, we cannot safely separa them, and so we must let them grow together until the harvest, which is judgme day.

There is an advantage to this system. The unbelievers and the curious are mo likely to come within the hearing of God's Word. The decision factor is much le evident; one is exhorted to be receptive to the tide of God's grace. The inclusiv aspect of the faith is emphasized, and the "gate is narrow and the road is hard (*Matthew 7:14*) aspect is less clearly addressed. Where salvation is seen as a finishe work, so that all we must do is realize it, the need somehow seems minimal.

Historically our denomination has held to what is called the "closed" churcl where belonging to Jesus is a prerequisite for belonging to the organization. Tha this is true can be seen in our per capita giving rate, which has often been ne the top among denominations. It indicates that giving, while still far from idea includes a sizable percentage of committed givers in the church membership.

It is vital to any church that the decision-making powers remain with tho who believe in Christ. The "open" church does not dare attempt such democrac the influence of the half-caring could thwart the church's purpose. So the power vested mostly in the clergy and in small groups. Conversely, we who give the rigl f choice freely can do so only within the group of those who are persuaded that sus is Lord. It is his wisdom that permits us to survive and grow.

The final dilemma is how to promote the concept of church membership to he point where the New Testament ideal is understood. Our individual-oriented ciety thinks of loyalty only as a means to an end; we defend our personal dependence fiercely. We often approach our church with a chip on our shoulder: e will not be coerced. We will not be submerged into the gray sameness of a roup. To teach the necessity of belonging to the body of Christ, to quote "you e not your own," (1 Corinthians 6:19) is to ask for a tremendous turnabout in ne's life.

The evangelical tradition, with its emphasis on the direct individual relationship ith God, is no help either. We have been so successful in crushing the idea of the urch as mediator that we have left it only a minor role. We hardly understand he doctrine of the kingdom because that group concept fits poorly with the dividual emphasis of evangelicalism.

But the voices from the New Testament are clear: as God's people we must eet together by his command and his empowering. And from that group must our forth, both corporately and singly, the fruits of the Holy Spirit. To make our forts efficient and applicable to our day, we must organize. We cannot accept the ild-parent relationship only; we are bound together as brothers and sisters. In he final analysis, we do not belong to ourselves but "to him who loves us and freed s from our sins by his blood." (*Revelation 1:5*) ❧

Chapter 6:
Christian Education

Study and discipleship are essential elements for growth in the Christian life. This chapter explores the nature and needs of a Christian Education program.

The Mind Needs the Spirit

1942. Written during Lincoln's last year at North Park Seminary.

Father, I must study now,
And I cannot work alone,
Without thee I am doomed to fail,
I have no power of my own;

Grant, Father, that thy blessing fall
On this attempt to wisdom find,
That others soon may learn of thee
From a humble, consecrated mind.

❧

Climate for Learning

2000. *Originally published on the Internet.*

Having previously chastised public education for its refusal (and it is a deliberate refusal) to provide the necessary climate or emotional posture to teach efficiently it is my duty to deal with the other, the beneficent, religious establishments which do not teach well either.

Whereas the public provided the subject matter but not the climate, so the religious pattern has the reverse trouble: they provide the loving, encouraging setting that is necessary, but they botch the subject matter.

Teaching in a church or in a Sunday School is provided by untrained volunteers and this is the root of the problem as well as its hope. The teacher says to herself "I'm no teacher, but my heart is right, and it is my duty to spread the gospel therefore since I am pressed to serve in this way, O.K., here I go. I know what the Bible says, I will tell them as faithfully as I can."

I have the feeling that the toddler is taught quite well, but that as the age of the student increases, the teaching gets worse.

In a church I recently served, I thought that adults should be asked to learn dutifully, with lessons that required thought and perhaps some homework; a real effort with a real result. I offered such a course, six sessions, where the material presented would not be allowed to just be poured on and then dried off. Six people accepted the challenge, but found themselves unable to attend more than once or twice. I tried, then shrugged; perhaps adults don't want to be taught.

It is amazingly dense of us all that we have allowed Sunday School to consist only of those who will listen but not try to retain, to tolerate but never be asked to act on what was learned. So poor a setup has had a poor result; In Christianity we are responsible for what we learn, to act on it. The New Testament makes it clear that knowing has no justification in itself; obedience must follow.

Then what? We can't hire professionals, and the Word must go out. What do we do? There are a few ideas that will help to compensate for lack of training.

1. The teacher must declare him or herself, that they are followers of Jesus Christ; that they love Him, and that they wish the same for those before them.

2. The New Testament Gospels teach us by narrative; what they did in the first century we should do in the twenty-first. That Jesus taught by stories was wonderful in its staying power; we remember the stories much better than the arguments.

3. The teacher must be faithful in attendance; each absence says that other things are more important to me.

4. The teacher must not try to simplify what is tremendously deep; she must resist the temptation to reduce the message to John 3:16 or the Sermon on the Mount or even the Apostles Creed. And she must not fake opinions about what she does not know.

5. We teach more by who and what we are than by what we say; our memories of long-ago teachers consists not in what they said, but the attitude, the serenity that reveals that we are humble followers of Christ. ❧

Let's Take a Look at Our Teaching

April 1989. *This article originally appeared in The Covenant Companion.*

The purpose of Christian education needs to be re-examined. Since Robe Raikes's first school until now, the schooling approach to Christian education h been considered not only a useful tool of the church, but lately has been thoug to be an integral part of faith itself, even a means of grace, and the foremost ar of outreach. It may even be asserted that by learning the Scriptures we come believe; the facts are the firm basis for faith. This view has been so taken for grant that we have not needed to review it; it is perfectly dear to nearly everybody.

But when these assumptions meet the test of experience, certainty turns in uncertainty. I think of those adult Sunday School classes some people attend f forty years without making an appreciable change in their habits. Our confirman after a more intense course of study, tend to disappear from the church. So mu of Bible study, however faithfully pursued, has an air of stagnation about it.

These failures, as well as many others, are readily blamed on the inhere sinfulness of the human race. We witnessed the best we could, and the rest is to God who gives the increase. We accept this percentage of failure as a matter course, and pray that the next lesson may be received by hearts more open to t Gospel.

But let me reopen this case which has been closed for so long. First, Christi education and Christianity are not synonymous. To know is not enough, b to know, to feel, and then to act is obligatory. By and for itself, the schooli approach to Christian education could lose its way. It could give light witho energy. It may fill the mind, but not transform the heart.

The need for absolute unity of information and action is stressed by the warnin of the New Testament in this regard. "But be doers of the word, and not mere hearers who deceive themselves." (*James 1:22*). "Whoever does not love does n know God, for God is love." (*1 John 4:8*). "And everyone who hears these wor of mine and does not act on them will be like a foolish man..." (*Matthew 7:2(* "Anyone, then, who knows the right thing to do and fails to do it, commits sir (*James 4:17*). "But those who look into the perfect law...being not hearers wh forget but doers who act — they will be blessed in their doing." (*James 1:25*).

But how can we follow our learning with the practice of our faith? Shall we confront someone as we leave the house of God? We cannot plan the circumstances of our day; we have no way of knowing what the next hour will bring. But can't we set up some deliberate exercise, role-playing, a bit of the world in miniature, hands-on activity that will help to bridge that critical gap? I am of the impression that in public schools explanation and demonstration take up one-third of the time, and the response, the doing, the practicing takes two-thirds of the time. Unless you can do it, they say, you don't know it. What does this say to our Sunday Schools, where often the explanation takes nearly 100 percent of the time?

The sanctity of our present set-up is so pervasive that we hardly dare to rethink these matters. And yet if we allow the accumulation of knowledge to become an end in itself, our efforts not only become ineffectual but tend to become a substitute for faith itself.

Learning about Christianity is a lot easier than being disciples of Christ. I know I tend to bask in the lesson at hand; it is so much easier than carrying a banner to an unbelieving world. In fact, I can get hooked on it. I will learn, and learn, and learn: "who are always being instructed and can never arrive at a knowledge of the truth." (*2 Timothy 3:7*)

We must reluctantly conclude that unless Christian education includes working out faith, it is likely to become ineffectual, or a hindrance, or even a substitute for the Gospel.

The medium-the aura in which the Bible and Christian education make sense-is the Holy Spirit. "But, as it is written, "What no eye has seen, nor ear heard, nor the human heart conceived, what God has prepared for those who love him" — these things God has revealed to us through the Spirit" (*1 Corinthians 2:9-10*). "When the Spirit of truth comes, he will guide you into all the truth" (*John 16:13*). Anyone who has read the Bible before and after conversion knows the difference — a pall of gloom with morose mystery beforehand, and a page vibrantly alive afterward. But how can we call upon the Spirit to help us succeed?

We must take for granted that the one who teaches possesses the in-dwelling Holy Spirit as a guiding force. Without the Spirit, futility reigns. The central task is to let the students participate in the Spirit, so that they can understand. But can we teach the Bible in the same way we could teach any other printed matter, with the same results?

In the first place, we learn best that which pertains to our own lives. The more relevance, the easier it is to learn; the mind is driven by the will. If we are dubious or uninterested, we will neither care nor understand. It follows then that the soul must first be awake. "Anyone who resolves to do the will of God will know whether the teaching is from God..." (*John 7:17*). This seems to indicate that willingness is a prerequisite to learning; obedience makes it clear. This is the opposite of secular learning, in which we ponder and understand before we act.

At this point it seems we have a dilemma: if we wait for obedience before we teach, how can we reach out? If on the other hand, we explain it to those who have no interest or intent, how in the world will they learn?

The only answer that presents itself is that the unbeliever is to be affected by the presence of believers — that the spiritual climate of the class penetrates the consciousness of the dubious and unwilling, and begins to clarify and illuminate. "For where two or three are gathered in my name, I am there among them." (*Matthew 18:20*). We could refer to this climate as the presence of the Holy Spirit, or we can call the group a little bit of the kingdom of God. If the flame burns brightly in some, the others are aware of its light and its influence. But someone must bring the flame if the common fire is to be lighted. In other words, the effectiveness of Christian teaching is partly dependent on the presence of committed Christians.

At this point I visualize a beleaguered teacher with a class of thirteen-year-old boys; a climate of sneer and disdain could easily prevail and make the advance of faith impossible. But bring three or four genuine Christians into the room. They would sit there, say little or nothing, but they would pray earnestly. The attitude of some of the boys would change. To the extent we can surround those we teach with love and prayer, to that extent they will listen and understand. This, as I read it, is God's promise.

Knowing this, we ought not, in imitation of the world's methods, place one faithful soul among a horde of doubters as a teacher. The rules for effective Christian education are the same as the recipe for soul winning: the Christian fellowship that welcomes and loves and cares. The King is best seen in his kingdom.

Let us consider Christian education from another angle-the method. Here we have borrowed heavily from secular education: its grade levels, its class periods, its knowledge of human development and maturity. For material that does not require a response of the will, nor involve the emotions, well and good — we yield to their wisdom. But because Christian education cannot be separate from the purpose of reconciliation to God, its method must be inherent in the faith itself.

In secular education we build from the ground up, fact upon fact, concept upon concept, each the foundation for the next idea, presenting each new fact in simplicity or complexity according to the maturity and level of the student. It is a edifice we build, buttressed by experiment and experience.

But Christianity is good news relayed from above — a discovery taught by each generation to the next, from ancient times until now, from parents to children, and the presence of the Holy Spirit, to whom time is not a factor, so that what we read of Bible times pertains today. As the hymn "Love Divine, All Loves Excelling" says, it is the "joy of heaven to earth come down." How shall we teach something so different?

There has to be a human chain of Spirit-filled people to pass on this illuminating flame. I doubt that the Spirit can reside in a book. Even God's Word is made clear by his Spirit, as noted in the hymn: "The Spirit breathes upon the Word, and brings the truth to light." I cannot impart what I do not possess.

Added to this factor is still another that could be puzzling: there is no graduation in Christian education. One does not come out at the end considered a Christian. In fact, the entry into the kingdom of God can occur at any point along the line; at any point in our knowing, we can know him, whom to know is life eternal.

I doubt that the rigorous separation of age groups is as efficient as we have thought it to be. It surely frustrates the "passing down the torch" idea. Dare we say that the interaction of the older with the younger, the saint and the inquirer, the discouraged with the jubilant, the experienced with the novice is not the way it was done in the New Testament? We have assumed that the unstructured crowds during Jesus' and Paul's time were due to their primitive societies. If all are at the same level, how does the living water flow from one to another?

I feel that we ought to emphasize tradition and continuity more than we do. Stressing the present, the age group, we have made ourselves relevant but without much anchor; considering ourselves wiser than the past makes us momentary with a tendency toward triviality. The sense of belonging, of passing along a vital gift to humankind, helps us to "run with perseverance the race that is set before us." (*Hebrews 12:1*)

85

The question of working out our faith is a difficult one. Only a small part of the Bible is a direct command or challenge. How shall I "do" the Twenty-third Psalm? How can I identify with Elijah on Mount Carmel? Some things we can do in class, such as sending cards or letters of comfort, welcome, and invitation. We can plan and promise to carry out that plan during the week. Assuming that our Sunday hours remain the same, the Sunday School is trapped between our tardy arrival and the worship service. Evening sessions have their limits — fatigue, darkness, and competing interests. So Sunday can only be a part of our total commitment.

But there are excellent opportunities to "...work out your own salvation..." (*Philemon 12:2*) by volunteering in community organizations. In the city where I live there are dozens of groups that display the love of Christ. Few are church sponsored, but I have no doubt that many of them are Christ inspired. Willingness to give many hours of one's time without apparent reward causes me to suspect that Jesus has been close by. Working in such groups, and then making clear that we do it in Christ's name-this should be an excellent way to witness. The action becomes the proof of our confession.

The Gospel is so unlike any other subject matter that we must re-examine each practice we have borrowed from secular education. One is focused on the mind only; the other aims at the will and heart. One is of this earth; the other is from above. One can be transmitted by books; the other needs a living example. One is locked into periods of time; the other is at once momentary and eternal. For one human effort is adequate; the other is empowered by the presence of God. ❧

Chapter 7:
Hymns for Worship

This chapter shows original music by Lincoln, along with hymn translations from Swedish, some of which were published in the denominational hymnal.

I Am Debtor

E. Lincoln Pearson

When Christ the Lord, who died that I might live, _____
If I can sing, I owe my Lord a song; _____
If I have faith, I must be faith-ful, true; _____
O Gra-cious God, from whom our bless-ings flow, _____

_____ For-gave my sin, I knew I must for-give; _____
_____ If I know right, I must re-sist the wrong; _____
_____ As God is love, I must love oth-ers too; _____
Teach me the vast-ness of the debt I owe! _____

_____ Be-cause He freed me by the cross He bore, _____
_____ If I can show the true and liv-ing way, _____
_____ For ev-ery prec-ious gift with-in me stored, _____
_____ And may this earth-en ves-sel, filled with praise, _____

_____ I am his grate-ful ser-vant e-ver-more _____
_____ May God be glo-ri-fied as I o-bey. _____
_____ I must give back in ser-vice to my Lord. _____
De-clare Thy ma-jes-ty through all my days. _____

Great Hills May Tremble

1946. *"Bergen må vika" by Lina Sandell, 1859. Original translation from Swedish, published in The Covenant Hymnal.*[2]

Great hills may tremble and mountains may crumble,
My lovingkindness remaineth secure,
Peace will I give to the contrite and humble,
Thus saith the Lord, and His promise is sure.

Teach me, O Lord, thy commandments to ponder,
Help me to heed them wherever I roam;
Waiting the day Thou shalt call me up yonder,
Trusting Thy promise to carry me home.

❧

When Toil Is Done, a Sabbath Rest is Waiting

1946. *"Sabbatsvila" by J. Fredrik Lundgren, 1884. Original translation from Swedish, published in The Covenant Hymnal.*[3]

When toil is done, a Sabbath rest is waiting
For God's own children in His mansions fair;
A Sabbath day, a glorious congregating
Of souls redeemed, eternal rest to share.

No griefs shall mar the bliss of that reunion,
For God Himself shall wipe all tears away,
And in the glory of that high communion
No trace shall be of heartaches or dismay.

A throng shall come from every tribe and nation
To stand in awe before the throne of God;
And with their song of grateful adoration
The Savior's name in joy forever laud.

When that eternal Sabbath morn is breaking
That now in faith we see through earth's dim haze,
O blessed Savior, speed my soul in making
Its journey home to join that song of praise.

❧

This is Our Covenant

February 12, 1984. *Original hymn text set to the hymn tune "Mit Freuden Zart".*

This is our covenant with God, the God of our salvation;
To serve as once our fathers served their bygone generation.
To being the gospel's saving grace to every land, to every race,
Their testament fulfilling.

This is our covenant with God, the Lord of all compassion,
That those who suffer grief and pain receive his consolation.
Held in the bosom of His care,
Quenched are the hurt and sorrow there,
His mercy everlasting.

This is our covenant with God, to search the sacred writings;
Teach its eternal truths abroad, sin-darkened pathways lighting.
To cherish what the Lord has said,
To partake of the Living Bread,
A manna for the pilgrim.

Should tyranny's unsparing hand declare our faith forbidden,
May Christ's disciples faithful stand
With strength that comes from heaven.
To tread where saints and martyrs trod —
This is our covenant with God,
Eternal life receiving.

❧

Childhood Faith

976. *Original translation from Swedish of the hymn "Barna Tro."*

In these days of doubt and pain, does your childhood faith remain?
Can you pray today that simple prayer again?
God, who holdeth children dear, let Thy little one draw near,
May I sleep tonight secure within Thy hand.

Refrain:
O for faith like a child! That bridges weary earth and heaven mild!
O for faith like the young,
Whose bright, believing song has just begun.

You may seek a guiding star in some distant land afar,
Making power or earthly gain your only goal,
But your tears of joy will flow when some childhood song you know
Will remind you of that harbor for your soul.

Refrain

Like a harbor in a storm, like a springtime turning warm
Was the peace and calm I felt at mother's knee,
All her earnestness and love seemed like blessing from above
When she prayed the Lord to guide and strengthen me.

Refrain

All the peace of childhood days, all the joys of simple praise,
Will be yours if you will kneel before the Lord;
For your calling on His name brings that childlike trust again,
You can sing anew with simple faith restored.

Refrain

❧

Christ the Lord is Risen

April 2, 1944. *An original translation from Swedish of the hymn "Kristus är Uppstånden."*

Christ the Lord is risen,
Praise Him, O my soul!
Christ the Lord is risen,
Him in song extol!
Death has lost its horror,
Gone its power to slay –
Heaven conquered hell, and
Rolled the stone away.

Refrain:
Sing then, weary pilgrim,
Christ is living still!
Granting life and eternal hope to
All who do his will.
Christ the Lord is risen,
This our greeting be;
Laud Him for the promise
Of Eternity.

Join in our rejoicing,
Come this Eastertide,
Join the triumph song that
Ever shall abide!
Victor over death, and
Sin, and fear, and shame;
Praise the risen Saviour,
Magnify His name.

Refrain

May the Lamb of God who
Died on Calvary,
Rise within your heart
To set your spirit free!
Free to tell his glory
Till some day above,
We shall sing the story
Of His wondrous love.

Refrain

❧

Christine is Coming

1942. *Original ranslation from Swedish of the hymn "Jesus Kommer" by J. A. Hultman.*

Christ is coming! Christ is coming!
Soon we hear the trumpet call;
In the brightness of his glory
We shall see the Lord of all.

Refrain:
May our lamps be burning brightly,
When he comes to claim his own,
That we may, with his beloved,
Enter our eternal home.

Are you ready, soul, to meet him?
Now prepared to meet your God?
Do you love the Saviour dearly,
Do you read his precious Word?

Refrain

Blest is he who waits his coming,
Blessed is the soul that yearn;
He shall gain a crown of glory
When the Risen Lord returns.

Refrain

Let me follow thee, O Jesus,
So that on life's farther shore,
I may find that peaceful heaven –
Place of rest forevermore.

Refrain

❧

Part III:
The Christian Life

Chapter 8:
Understanding the Faith

This chapter explores with a magnifying glass the mystery of the interaction between Jesus Christ and the believer.

Souls of Men

1941. *Written while Lincoln was student at North Park Seminary.*

I walked by the shore of a placid sea
As dust crept over the strand
And I stooped, half-dreaming, and wrote my name
With a stick in the yielding sand.

I came again in the morning light
And stopped, but looked in vain;
For wind and wave had come at night,
And washed away my name.

'Tis gone, I said to myself, and yet
The memory still remains;
Is it true that the sands of life will shift,
And only the soul will gain?

Yes, all of the labor that hands can spend
Will pass with the sand and clay;
So let me work with the souls of men
That endure for a longer day.

❧

Originally, It Was Called Sin

1998. *First published on the Internet.*

The human race has a serious, even fatal flaw. It cannot live up to its potential. It knows that the flaw is there. It recognizes a standard which must have been meant for us, but the most heroic efforts to live up to that standard are doomed to fail. And we know that we fail.

This is a curious situation. Why do we seem to be programmed for something which is forever beyond us? Does the cat feel guilty because it cannot fly? Does the puppy feel ashamed because it doesn't live in a tree? Of course not.

If we believe in the God of the Bible, we cannot visualize Him as putting into our design something negative, an angst which we cannot resolve, a worry that we cannot put to peace. Unless — and this a long shot — there was a time when this dilemma was not there, when we did live up to our full potential.

So then we are talking history. It was good before, but bad afterward. That we know the good was there - that is our standard. That it doesn't work now - that's proof that we have lost something. Whatever happened, it happened to the whole human race; No tribe, no century, has been excluded.

Suppose we visit an old farm where a friend of ours lives. The welcome, the growing crops, the machinery, the toil are all self-explanatory. There are a few old buildings; one of them is empty. Why? A granary, perhaps; no longer fit to use, but the building is still there. It makes me wonder: isn't there a room in our souls that we can't use any more? Some compartment that definitely was in use, but now is vacant? A room called righteousness, from which we have been driven?

That begins to sound like the story of Adam and Eve, and how they were driven from the Garden of Eden. The story of the fall of our first parents is much clearer, much more effective than my attempt to explain the situation.

The account of Adam and Eve and their sin tells us the origin of our original sin. The story fascinates me, because first of all, that it happened, I have no trouble believing it; God passes it on to me, and I rest in it. Second, this story is true in a vast sense, as though Adam and Eve were projected across the sky, and beneath it words written, Disobedience Leads to Tragedy. Or in an even greater sense, this story is written into the universe itself, Estrangement from God Leads to Sorrow.

This, then, is original sin. Sin takes many forms, but its source is the same. What weakness we inherit, that is original sin. How we act because of it I would call plain sin. Another distinction also: When we fail in spite of our good intentions and good will, that must be original; when we will to do evil, that I would not call original sin. When there is a subjective decision to be made, and we choose what seems to be the best course, but still it turns out wrong, The Apostle Paul says, "Now if I do what I do not want, I agree that the law is good. So I find it to be a law that when I want to do what is good, evil lies close at hand." (*Romans 7: 20-21*)

Original sin can be thought of as only potential — as a latent weakness which does not exist until the mistake is made. Is it not resident until you see it come out? A mother dresses her two-year-old for the party; the little boy is clean, right? But it takes the mother another half hour to dress, and the little boy heads for the dirt in the back yard. Dirty in no time. Now, was the dirt in the boy at first, showing itself slowly, or do we refuse to acknowledge the dirt until the contact with the mud is made?

The new political office-holder finds a few thousand dollars unmarked. Is the evil already there, or does it exist only when that office-holder has spent it renovating the office with luxury beyond reason?

We cannot overcome this sin by ourselves. Even with all flags flying in pursuit of a good cause - we lose. When God saw that our best efforts with best intentions did not suffice, He sent Jesus. Only Jesus can change our souls enough to rescue us from this persistent loss. That one building block of human nature is missing; we have no god-stuff with which to fill it.

The car stalls. It's obvious; it must be the battery. The battery is charged, we are on our way. Again it stalls. It was the alternator, the thing that makes the electricity for the car. There is a part of us that only God can make; we thought we needed some recharging, but no; we need Him who makes the power we live by. ❧

Maturity and Freedom

1997. *Originally published on the Internet.*

So you want to be free? So do we all. But the question of being free is a complex one, even though it may not seem to be so at first. There are several requirements. But if there are requirements, how can I be free? Let me tell you.

First, there are the requirements of the body. You are bound to live inside it, and any feeling you may have must come from your body. Of course declaring yourself free from caring for it means illness or even death. The child who eats only candy, or refuses to limit the amount of food intake, will suffer eventually. Your body also means that you are in one place at a time, not somewhere else. You cannot insist that you will be in Bulgaria in an hour's time.

Related to the body requirement is the use of time. Just so much day, so much night. If you cheat at one end, it is deducted from the other. Students who go to college are delighted that they can stay up as long as they want, only to find that doing so has its penalty. Freedom, yes, but only within certain boundaries.

Another limitation of our freedom is that society demands certain things of us.

The plane leaves when scheduled, not before. The office-holder is secure until the next election, in spite of our seething. The store closes. A strike, and our package does not come. The neighbor's radio keeps us awake. We missed the trash collection schedule. The friend is sick, and cannot accompany us. The snow in our driveway should have been plowed by now. So much for our freedom.

There is another restriction: what shall I do with my life? If I go north, spending time there, I have left south behind. If I change curriculum in mid-course, much time and effort have been wasted. Obviously I cannot keep changing my mind in the name of freedom. I must choose well, and soon; I am not free to do nothing, or to vacillate.

There may exist a mental block that could hinder me. I tend to choose my alternatives from that which I have already experienced, and that limitation could be a tragedy. There is much more to taste and sample. Sometimes it seems that four years of college are a waste of information, most of which is forgotten. But that is not the point: the point is that in those classes, wider horizons become visible there is more richness to life than you thought. And that realization stays with the graduate; you can usually tell the difference.

Freedom is restricted by our immaturity; we cannot enjoy what we do not know. The question arises: does freedom presuppose responsibility? The New Testament says "yes." We have been given freedom; we must give back. We are capable; our freedom is to be used for others. We were intended for a certain kind of life; to live our life as it was intended is our greatest reach, our freedom.

To discover that life has a fulcrum, a pivot, a point from which all things make sense it tremendously freeing. If you know from what point the numbers on the map are measured, then it all makes sense. There is one point at which all the tumblers in the lock agree; this is the open door. That we were intended to be in constant contact with the Infinite; what a discovery that is! The phonograph record makes sense only if the center rules; then the music arrives. The ultimate freedom is to live as we were intended to live; the Creator is our fulfillment. ❧

Our Half-Truths

1999. *Originally published on the Internet.*

We all have little bits of wisdom that become a part of our religion. Sometimes they are half-truths that need explanation and perhaps refutation. For a small-group meeting I offer these half-truths for discussion, in the hope that we can by contrast come up with something fully true and useful.

1. The Bible was written long before civilization emerged, and so the primitive injunctions will need the tempering and correction of modern day scholarship.

2. Religion seems to refuse any correction necessary for the modern mind to grasp. Fortunately popular opinion serves to point out how necessary it is to keep up to date.

3. Several of our genius churchmen have discovered facts and impressions that escaped the searching of twenty previous centuries, so bringing a new and positive note to the Scriptures.

4. We should be more patriotic; our victory is a victory for God.

5. Everything seems to be wrong with Africa. Obviously God favors North America. For a hundred or more years, it has been the Promised Land.

6. I belong to the true church, so they will take care of my soul.

7. I won't eat pork. Haven't you read Leviticus? This gives me good health.

8. Most of the world's trouble is lack of money, so I give money.

9. Religious requirements should be reasonable; none of this fasting stuff.

10. Jesus was a revolutionary. Come join our revolutionary party.

11. Our church is the largest building of all; we are very successful.

12. How do we get to know the truth? We take a vote.

13. Our pastor is a man of God, so we don't dare disagree with him.

14. It's not what you believe, but how strongly you believe it.

15. If I'm a good guy, God will take me in. Better me than the sinners.

16. If God made sex, what can be wrong with it? Gotta keep humanity going.

17. It doesn't pay to try so hard. Success is mostly a matter of luck.

18. The doctor who kills unborn babies - does he deserve to live himself?

19. You get out of religion what you put into it, as with all things.

20. I don't owe anybody anything; I'm a self-made man.

21. Of course we are supposed to love ourselves most of all.

22. I "do unto others." (*Matthew 7:12*) That's the whole Bible in a nutshell.

23 If I place a bet and win, what's wrong with that? Should I lose?

24. If you believe science, then you don't believe in God.

25. Capitalism is Christian; everybody gets an even chance.

26. Whatever I do, I know that God will forgive it.

27. The ungodly won't listen to a presentation of the gospel.

28. It's too hard to change anybody's beliefs; just love them instead.

29. Nobody wants me to pry into their troubles. ✣

I Worship My Creator

2002. *Originally published on the Internet.*

There once was in me a mental separation between the redemptive God and th Creator-God, but no longer. To the extent that I have been allowed to peek int the wonders of the world we live in, the more I find reason for increasing praise.

The beauty, the designs, the complexities, and the reliabilities of the worl around us overwhelm our understanding and cry out for acceptance. I offer thes categories as representing the way I worship my Creator.

Reliability. Though we are affected by our emotions and conflicting thoughts nature around us is reliable. The length of the day and year are absolutel predictable. The plant world replies to our efforts endlessly. The distances fron one place to another stay the same; the seasons are regulated by a system we onl partly understand. The North Star stays in its place. So accustomed are we to dependable world that to point out the fact seems naive. The same God can hea our prayers with the same faithfulness.

Beauty. Why are flowers beautiful? Why are there millions of blossoms w shall never see? Why the endless splashes of color in nature? And why do humar beings recognize color? The same God made both us and nature; isn't the beaut for us? Why does color affect our moods? We realize now that there are million of colors; they are part of an intricate system designed by the Creator. So when th white cumulus clouds float against a background of blue, how can I say that this i all chance; that it is all without meaning?

Design. Why do the petals fit all around the flower? Why do grandma's nos and father's chin and mother's brown eyes all fit into the baby's face? Why do th atoms know where they belong? Why do snowflakes base their designs aroun the number six? Why do rainbows use predictable colors? How does the blade o grass know which way is up? How does a leaf know how it should look? How d the branches of a pin oak know at what angle to emerge? How does the trunk of tree know how much load it can bear? How many teeth will a lower jaw have; wh decided that? How can an egg have in it all the qualities of the bird it will become Who designed the wings of a bird, specialized to fit the eventual flying habits o the bird? Who figured out the scales of the elements? Does light always travel a the same speed? Who knows the human body completely?

The examples of design are endless, and their source is God.

Complexity. I have seen charts of the nervous system of the human body; how intricate! I see movies of schools of little fish swimming in formation, and I realize that the number of fish involved is impressive, but the more impressive is the guidance systems which make something so small to be so complete. I see the stars on a summer night; what I see is a miniature map of systems so complex that no chance could have caused it, and so great and so distant that it boggles the mind. I see the fingers of a pianist in concert, and marvel at the minds that express so complex a movement. Is there any other answer but that a Supreme Being has designed this possibility?

Greatness. The scale of God's works is awe-inspiring; from the atom to the galaxy. Human beings can only handle a bit along that scale, and that reality reaches far beyond us in both directions is reason for awe and worship. And God's greatness is not only in size, but in its nature. Why do we have electricity? Yes, we may admire what people have done with electricity, but why does it exist? Why is it so transportable? Why does it keep its nature? Why the certain speed? We who use it unthinking ought to bow before the evidence of this wonder, and the God who first fashioned it, and keeps it within its bounds.

Purpose. Scientists come up with a steady stream of oddities, of deviations God has made in the general creation to make it a livable world for humankind. The distance from the sun - the correct amount of heat; the rotation of the earth that makes the day a usable length; the revolution of the earth around the sun for the seasons (and available crops to fit the season.) The certain place in the solar system where the earth will not wander; the rays that protect us from the sun; the air, in addition to breathing, to reflect the light of the sun; the correct mix of gases in the air, with the right and trouble-free amount of oxygen; the way plants take in carbon dioxide and offer oxygen to us. God set the conditions under which we may thrive; apparently He loves his creatures and He must have a purpose for us.

That purpose can only be one thing: that his children share with each other the ualities and substances which the earth and life provide, making life good for all f us. This purpose has been thwarted by a wrong and permanent attitude in all of us - sin, whereby we harm each other rather than help.

So to work against that self-destructive attitude, God gives us a chance to come out of it. He sends Jesus to offer an attitude which takes away our tendency to destroy each other; simply by accepting God as ruler of one's life one can feel a loving spirit, a cleansing feeling, by which we discard our destroyer role, and activated by communication with God, can begin in our small way to clean up life around us. This is God's purpose; this is why I worship my Creator. ❧

On Being Too Close

2001. *Originally published on the Internet.*

The trouble I have had in understanding the Christian Faith is that I have been too close. You can understand better the height of a building when you can see it among other buildings. If you stand back, you can see the whole in proportion to its parts; you can then realize that where you are is not the whole; the rest of it must come into view. Then you know.

I grew up in the middle of it, so I did not see its boundaries or its restrictions. I grew up as an obedient unquestioning pietist; was there anything else? We sang the songs about the wounds of the dying Savior; that was O.K., wasn't it? I was part of a group apart; was there any horizon that I had missed? I realize now that I missed plenty.

I interacted with those who had not committed themselves to Christ, but felt that their lives were quite decent. It puzzled me that one could be good, as good as the believers, but lack the name. I know now that their apparent goodness was a gift of those near them who believed — they were absorbing the effects of the Spirit — but where I stood, I had no way to tell.

Then came a time when in my drug store job I was inundated by crass and ugly unbelief; it was a cold rain on my sensitive and innocent soul. I winced and somehow hid; I had no way to answer something so overwhelming. Since I have had the opportunity to back away and see from afar, I realize that these people have no answers; it is braggadocio and ignorance combined that made up their answers to the meaning of life. The rest of life shone on the situation, and revealed its poverty.

Then came the years of college and seminary when I heard that what I had believed was much richer than I thought. But in the background was the unspoken understanding that our efforts were doomed to fail; that evil was so much stronger that our hopes lay in secluding ourselves from the harshness of the cruel day round us. Being set apart, a favorite thought, included being set apart from the struggles that were out in the world. A little bit of the kingdom seemed so sweet, a preferable alternative to the debate in the marketplace.

Then the years of ministry another dimension; when I stood back I saw that the struggle between good and evil existed even in the parish; there was no place to hide. It took a long time of being hurt (and hurt by so-called "God's people") that I could at last see the scope and the power of the devil amongst us. Practice of the faith was still being snowed under in spite of the niceness that called me pastor.

But at last maturity has come for me. But I'm not sure of that; am I standing far enough back? The tremendous effect that Jesus Christ has had on history had made me sure that He is effective for our day. I have looked up enough from the Scripture pages to see how much Jesus is doing in our time, in our nation, in our efforts to heal the sick, to carry out an effective plan of education, to make our laws effective, to change hatred to love, selfishness to loving service, from hate groups to inclusive servants, from cheating toward absolute honesty; from competition to cooperation in serving our country; to healing the family, and making family life lovable; to break down barriers behind which we had left others out; to make a tremendous difference in the society and nation. ❧

Chapter 9:
Living the Faith

Faith should be practiced — applied in our daily lives in our thoughts and through our actions. This chapter examines some of the challenges believers face as they put "feet on their faith."

Faith for Blue Mondays

1941. *Written while Lincoln was a student at North Park Seminary.*

Lord of Morning and of light of day,
Give me strength to live, I pray.
Bestow thy care and loving keeping,
Now in working as in sleeping.
I do not ask an easy road,
But strength from thee to bear the load,
And whether pain or gladness come,
I will follow Christ, thy son.

❧

Full Membership Is Required

1998. *Originally published on the Internet.*

Though I grew up within three miles of Lake Erie, I never learned to swim wel
Two reasons: Our family never owned a car, and my Mother was afraid for me;
son of good friends had drowned about six months before I was born. In fact, m
name Lincoln came from that boy who was drowned.

I remember, sometime before I was ten years old, pretending to swim b
paddling correctly but keeping one foot on the bottom, or near it. That metho
was futile, of course; I never learned to trust myself to the buoyancy of the wate

We use our Christian faith like that; we know that it is marvelous, that w
believe in Christ, but want to keep the old system of trusting only ourselves at th
same time. That way we can have the best of both worlds, we think.

It doesn't work, of course. When Jesus says, "Follow me," (*Matthew 4:1*
and we are supposed to rely on Him only — that's too hard for our hedonist
generation. There's got to be a way to have both; but it appears that in th
compromise we get neither.

The Gospel promises us that we will be taken care of, and theoretically we agre
that it is true. We want to be lifted out of the pit of self, but we bring along
ladder, just in case.

The truth is, in spite of the promise that we will be taken care of, we feel poo
So we scratch for more money; we don't feel secure. Now if God really took ca
of us, if we felt that our Father was rich in houses and lands, then we could fe
secure. But there is no half-and-half status, no foot on the bottom, so we are not i
the kingdom with that ploy. We must trust in God fully in order to feel his han
under us; full membership in His family is required. We outsmarted ourselves.

We feel alone. The gospel speaks of great fellowship; and that Jesus said, "An
remember, I am with you always, to the end of the age." (*Matthew 28:20*) But ou
faith was not intended to be an individual thing; we are to be a part of the famil
Unless you are stranded alone on a secluded island, this means you. It appears tha
this fellowship which is to conquer our loneliness comes about partly with ou
own effort; we must reach out to each other.

114

If you read the Bible, the urge to be a part of a church will come to you naturally. The fellowship offer is good and real, but we must consent to it.

We feel cheated. Life isn't fair. And we covet the things that others have. We even regret that we have not spent more energy trying to earn more money. It is a feeling that we all have had. The promise of the Gospel is not that we shall have as much; it points out that life is a journey, and what we have is our luggage. Too much, and we lose life's purpose while we gather things around us. We cannot savor the day we have; only the tomorrow with more things will be good enough for today.

Our biggest fear is death; so many of our worries center around it. The gospel makes clear - we shall receive life eternal if we believe. But when we watch others die, we can't tell if they have received their reward or not. Even if we could delay death, it is still certain. If I could believe that I shall live again, life would be a lot different. If I could rest in that assurance, it would be wonderful; no dark valley, no extinction.

If we cast ourselves on His mercy, all the promises come true in Him. ❧

The Fruit Needs the Tree

2001. *Originally published on the Internet.*

In the early part of the twentieth century, Christianity was prevalent enough so that its cause and its effect were simultaneous, and we could not separate them. The general populace was dimly aware of the niceness that was the air in which faith existed, but no definite division could be ascertained.

We who went to church did not consider the effects of believing; we just knew that God was there, and we must get right with Him. Then came the long decline; we had assumed that our sailboat could move without the wind. And when the storm approached, we were found to be ill prepared.

For discussion let us divide the faith into cause and effect, into source and destination, into giver and receiver. God is the source, and we receive. Or God is the force, and we are affected. The whole point of this essay is that the believer has nothing until God gives it; that unless there is a transfer of the life-giving effect from above to us below, any attempt to display what we do not have is impossible.

For now, let us say that the proof of the effective faith consists of all the good qualities with which we are familiar: love, joy, peace, longsuffering, patience, goodwill, kindness, gratitude, calmness, humility, hope, forgiveness, willingness, friendship, inner strength, and many more. This list can not be limited, because God is all love, all goodness, and he shows Himself in infinite number of forms.

The unbelieving world thinks that these qualities are random, that anyone at any time can acquire them. That's not all bad; at least most of them are in favor of these in society. But when we look for godlike results in a godless situation, they aren't there. My point is that the good qualities of character require a connection with heaven. You cannot be loving unless love is pouring into you. You cannot be sufficiently patient unless you are receiving the strength and the grace of God.

And that connection must be quite continuous. We are not battery-operated in the sense we get a good dose of God which will last us a long time; the beneficial result occurs only when we are "plugged in" to God. Jesus said it best, "...apart from me you can do nothing." (*John 15:5*) That means that Jesus the presence makes possible Jesus the integrity or the kindness.

It means, and history has shown us, that giving to the poor without the presence of Jesus is futile; our nation has tried it. But the unbeliever still thinks he can be nice if he wants to, but he doesn't want to. Much of our main-line religion has tried to show great qualities without the heaven connection, and their memberships have plummeted.

They love the fruit, but they are not connected with the Christ from whom this life-giving ability comes. That's why the hour of prayer is essential; what we need for the crisis comes from Him. ❧

Millions for Christ, Or None?

1998. *Originally published on the Internet.*

The number of people who call themselves Christians is considerable. Som
estimates talk about millions, even 40, 50, or 60 millions who say that they ar
born again. Yet we get the impression that these millions have very little effect o
the lifestyle of the average citizen.

Looking to the New Testament for an answer to this quandary, we see that th
early Christians were a small minority, yet they achieved a tremendous influenc
on the Roman Empire. We have no alternative to saying that whatever they had
we do not have; whatever an individual in the first century could accomplish fo
God, now hundreds or thousands cannot do.

The life of Jesus, his example, his teaching, and his sacrifice is as clear at it eve
was; indeed clearer, because our information systems are superb compared to thos
of earlier centuries.

So what is wrong, terribly wrong? It is something so close to us that we hav
not held it in front of our eyes to evaluate it. "The word is near you, on your lip
and in your heart." (*Romans 10:8*) So let us search our hearts. We have mad
a compromise with the world around us, a compromise so pervasive that it n
longer comes into our conscious thought. And looking everywhere but there, w
find no answer.

Let's begin with our envy, our covetousness, and our idolatry. It is assumec
is it not, that when the new appliance comes on the market, the new means c
transport, the new fabric, the new means of entertaining ourselves, that we have t
have it? Of course. For a while it is optional, but not for long. We must budget ou
finances or somehow earn more; we must have it. It is with no pang of conscienc
that we enjoy it. And then it becomes necessary.

Take the microwave, for example. A great invention. But before the microwav
was invented, did you long for it? Were you ashamed before your neighbor
that you did not have one? Were you saving for it? Were you happy before th
invention came on the scene? And if you were O.K. before it came, were you i
need of it? Are my questions irksome?

118

Our apparent need for something new, then, is heavily caused by envy and covetousness. This keeping up with the Joneses is a sin which has us in its grip so powerfully that our God-consciousness does not even compete. Our weakness in the Gospel duty is hamstrung by that dependence.

Of course God allows us to have goods, provided that we love the Lord with all our heart, and all our soul, and with all our mind. Our prevalent consumerism prevents that, and shows that we do not trust God's care.

If we are willing to spend our uncommitted money so completely that any emergency finds us over our heads, we have not accepted God's guidance and care.

We should deliberately limit our standard of living so that a part of our income is ready for giving generously to the Lord's work. Until we are willing to be freed from the envy and covetousness that fills our society, we risk having the Lord say to us, "I never knew you; go away from me, you evildoers." (*Matthew 7:23*) ❧

Here for This Reason

1998. *Originally published on the Internet.*

The ministry of Jesus was drawing to a close. The pressure of hatred from the temple leaders was intensifying. Yet Jesus knew, according to His Father's plan, He must give his life to fulfill it. That some Jews had come to the feast and were asking about him presented a divide - an opportunity to turn aside from His Father's will and perhaps be accepted beyond the bounds of Jewry.

"Now my soul is troubled." Jesus said, "And what should I say — 'Father, save me from this hour'? No, it is for this reason that I have come to this hour." (*John 12:27*)

The crisis was clearly stated. Death lay ahead, but so did purpose; everything depended on staying the course. That moment of obedience made all of the previous ministry valid. So great the difficulty; so great the purpose to be fulfilled.

There are pivotal points in all our lives. That moment when we choose at the fork in the road is critical; it determines what will follow, and it validates what has preceded it. These hours of our crisis turn out to be moral choices; the more difficult they are, the more crucial they turn out to be.

Notice that difficulty and importance come simultaneously; the agony of having to choose is proof of the crisis. What shall my attitude be toward my parents? Shall I go out for the team? Does this moment determine what my major shall be, and so also my occupation?

Shall I take this job, which has minimal chance for advancement but is comfortable? Shall I travel this year, and so "find myself?" Is this girl the obvious choice for a wife, or is she the kind who will rant and rave to get her way?

By what kind of inner measure am I making these choices? Greed will lead me astray; so will the sex drive. What part do my parents play in this? Will their advice prepare me only for their past generation? The ultimate decision is made not so much by the circumstances at hand as by what I really am, down deep.

If Jesus looked back to the purpose of his ministry, the choice was obvious. Even when He said, "Father, save me from this hour," (*John 12:27*) it did not change the clear precedence that obedience called for.

The moves that make our destiny are prepared for by many years of firm purpose. As we travel down the toll road, there are many turnoffs, but we are not confused by all of them; maybe the one nearest our destination. If on the sea we chart our course by heading toward 175 degrees, it is to be noted that that heading is dependent on our certainty that north is north, and does not deviate.

In the same way there is a temporary heading, but it is dependent ultimately on some celestial certainty - that the polar star will always be there as our guide.

God is the ultimate sense; if your choice leads out of His kingdom, that will be tragic, even if the job is a dream job. You see, as on the sea of life you head for what the centuries have shown to be God-approved, there are thousands of choices within His will. Which wave we confront is minimal; what star we seek is all-important. ❧

How're Your Windshields?

August 1, 1973. *This article originally appeared in The Covenant Companion.*

Sometimes our meticulously planned vacations turn out to be disappointing and frustrating experiences. We get where we're going and back all right; we spend the allotted time dutifully; we buy the most popular equipment; we sun ourselves doggedly, determined to get our money's worth. But all the while, it seems, we have to keep telling ourselves that this is fun. After all, don't other people seem to be enjoying it?

That's wrong! Somehow the pleasurable sensations the situation should provide are not getting through to the center of our being. There's a barrier between what our eyes see and what our souls feel-between our senses and our truest selves.

Perhaps we miss the point of vacation because we concentrate so much on the experience that we forget to prepare ourselves inwardly for it. We are great on "doing" things but poor on knowing why.

When wrong motives and negative emotions control us, experiences that could be wholesome often go sour. Here are some examples:

The uncle who carries a dozen assorted grudges shows up at the family reunion. How can he greet and embrace his relatives warmly?

A hijacker stands with his gun pointed at the pilot's head as the huge jet crosses over the Rocky Mountains. Can any of the grandeur of creation below get through in that setting?

Can a person who is steeped in indulgence ever really hear the fragile beauty of a song sung by little children?

When someone in your family is undergoing emergency surgery, can you really enter into that TV comedy in the waiting room of the hospital?

Can the driver who is fleeing from the scene of a hit-and-run accident enjoy the cool of the summer night as he speeds down the road?

And can a man bent on keeping up with everything really perceive and enjoy the gifts he has in house and home, wife and children?

We inevitably view the outer world through the eyeglass of our motives and the windshield of our emotions. What we do must be filtered through what we are. So, if your eye is healthy, your whole body will be full of light." (*Matthew 6:22*) Life is always resplendent to the pure in heart. But a wrong turn of the soul ruins our fun because it muddies our windshield. "Rather, your iniquities have been barriers between you and your God, " Isaiah says. (*Isaiah 59:2*)

Only a heart in touch with the Creator is aware of his creation. "See, I am making all things new." (*Revelation 21:5*) That's the Bible's way of saying that restoring communication with the Father tends to restore communication with the world that he has made.

A person who drives his auto under the stress of a strong negative emotion is said to have "tunnel vision." What he feels shuts out much of what he sees. Absorbed with himself, his world closes down narrowly around him.

Vacationing can get like that. The anxieties involved in preparation, the inexorable timetables, the frustrations of delay, the irritation with fellow-travelers, the ill temper of fatigue, the extra self-indulgences, the dismay at encountering additional expense — all these indicate a false faith that we are the gods running the show. No wonder we are left spent and undone when the pieces of our ill-ordered little world don't quite fit!

But let's not get discouraged, as though everything were hopeless. If we relinquish control of our lives to the Almighty again, tranquility and real joy can return. He who came to give life more abundantly is still the source of that basic rightness which makes the outer world fresh and clean to those with eyes to see. Whenever you look to him, your sense of perspective will return; so will your joy in living. ❧

Point the Way

November 1941. *Written while Lincoln was a student at North Park Seminary.*

Lord of Harvest, did you call to me
Today, when all the day's noise and din
Obscured thy pleading? Did my sin
Becloud the thin horizon of my soul?
Be patient, Lord, and speak to me again
With tone imperative. How well I know
The man beside me needs thy gracious love
To lift him from despair. Both he and I
Shall feel the sweet release from inward pain.
For mine, the pang of uselessness
Will curse my vacant day. O Lord of Harvest,
Speak to me again, and point the way.

❧

Make Thy Purpose Known

November 1941. *Written while Lincoln was a student at North Park Seminary.*

This day that thou shalt give me, loving Father,
I give it back to thee with all my will;
If I have any song or love within me,
These too are thine, and I am waiting still
To follow where thy hand shall lead me –
The bitter pathway of a shadowed valley,
A lonely wand'ring far from home,
Or simply waiting – God, what e'er it be,
Take thou my hand, and make thy purpose known.

Chapter 10:
Love and Marriage

In this chapter Lincoln's gift for poetry is evident in these tender poems written to his wife, and poems for the weddings of friends and family members.

God Gave Me You, Dorothy

1945. *Written for Dorothy Carlson, Lincoln's bride-to-be.*

God gave our hearts, where love and peace may dwell,
God gave our homes, dear, and joys no tongue can tell,
God gave his temple, where hope and faith renew,
And then to make my spirit sing,
God gave me you.

❧

For Dorothy Carlson

1945. *Written for Lincoln's bride-to-be.*

When first I heard that God above
Had called you by His voice of love
To serve Him all thy days, and thou
Didst yield to Him, and so didst vow,
There came to me this thought divine –
God chose you to be mine!
God chose you to be mine!

From that day forth, but God hath known
How great my love for thee hath grown!
Until with fondest joy today
I take thee to my heart for aye!
O may this truth our lives entwine –
God chose you to be mine!
God chose you to be mine!

O sweetheart, may this be our prayer
That God will keep us in His care
As we fulfill our solemn vow
To do His sovereign will, and now
May memory the day enshrine
God chose you to be mine!
God chose you to be mine!

ॐ

Stay by My Side

1945. *Written for Dorothy Carlson shortly before their wedding.*

When thou are mine, O love, our joy fulfilling,
And by the years our faithfulness be tried,
I only ask, though hope or grief be calling,
Stay by my side, O love, what e'er betide,
Stay by my side, O love, stay by my side!

Though life seems long, with every day revealing
A thorny path from dawn to eventide –
I count it all my joy, because I love thee,
Stay by my side, O love, what e'er betide,
Stay by my side, O love, stay by my side!

And if the winds of fate shall bring me kindness,
If life is good, and fortune smile beside,
Still is my love for thee my greatest gladness,
Stay by my side, O love, what e'er betide,
Stay by my side, O love, stay by my side!

❧

Radiant Song

1945. *Written and sung by Lincoln at his wedding to Dorothy Carlson.*

Darling, my bride, here at your side,
Great is my rapture today;
That I should find love so sublime
Lighting my future way.

Refrain:
Sweetheart, will you come with me,
And love me through the years;
Share both sad and joyous hours,
All my hopes and tears;

Sweetheart, will you seek with me,
Faith so pure and strong,
That at last our lives will be
One in radiant song.

Refrain

May the Lord give courage to live,
Grace for the burdens we bear,
Hearing us now fervently vow,
Blessing the love we share.

Refrain

❧

I Give Thee This Heart of Mine

June 8, 1942. *For the wedding of Lincoln's friends Rodney North and Jean Ackley.*

You were a dream in bygone years,
My angel of reverie,
Vision more cherished than words can say –
A beautiful melody;
You are my rapture of love today,
Pride of my inner shrine;
Let me but worship thy loveliness –
And give thee this heart of mine!

You are tomorrow's radiant song,
The sweetest that ear has known;
You are my peace in the tumult strong,
The light of our humble home.
Yours is my life in coming years,
All my devotion thine;
Yours is my future of joy and tears –
I give thee this heart of mine!

❧

Fragrant Hours

1942. To the tune of "My Rosary," for Lincon's friend Elvera Hafstrom's wedding.

The faith I bring to thee, dear heart,
Shall ever deep and constant be,
And everlasting as the verdured hills
My love for thee, my love for thee.

The splendor of a starlit sky,
The calmness of an evening prayer,
Portray for me the life of love,
That you and I shall share.

O memories of fragrant hours!
O hope of bliss that is to be!
These crown my day of joy, yet greater far
Abideth love, forever, my love for thee.

❧

This Sacred Hour

May 1941. *For Lincoln's sister Helen Pearson's wedding to Rube Ostrom.*

Gracious, Loving Father of Mankind
Look down with favor on this sacred hour,
And on these thy children, who just now,
Have pledged undying love to one another.
May thy benediction be upon them –
Let thy boundless grace enfold them always.
May their faithfulness to one another
Bring them to a deeper faith in thee.
In the years that lie before, protect them;
May happiness abide within their home.
And if adversity should come, then grant
That they may face it unafraid together,
Remembering these solemn vows today.

❧

Chapter 11: Family Life

This chapter's poems and essays are an intimate expression of appreciation of the joys of a loving Christian family.

Grant Us Thy Blessing

1940. Written during Lincoln's years as a student at North Park Seminary.

Father, grant us from above
Thy blessings on these gifts of love,
And teach us to ever thankful be
For countless mercies, friends, and thee.

❧

Each New Morning

1940. *Written while Lincoln was a student at North Park Seminary.*

Early in life's years, at each new morn,
Ere I would leave the home for school or play,
At mother's side I breathed this brief petition,
To ask my Lord to guide me through the day:

Father, guard me from all sin today,
Keep me close to thee, lest I should stray,
From gloomy vales of evil may I turn,
For truth and kindness of the heart I yearn
To see thy love shine clear upon my way,
Father, guard me from all sin today.

Still, though years have flown, and I have gone
To tread the thoroughfare of life alone,
I meet the Lord of Life at each new dawning,
And pray the simple prayer I learned at home:

❧

Father's Day

1938. *Written by Lincoln Pearson to his father.*

My Dad: It's Father's Day again
And of late I've thought of you,
How much you've done for me, your son,
Working many long years through;
You've toiled with greatest fortitude
Through grimy, tiring days,
To earn for me a victory
Without a thought of praise.
Through worry and discouragement
You swung the sledge and shoveled coal,
And brought a bag of candy home —
A token of a loving soul.
I won't forget your trust in me,
Though I seemed so worthless then,
Making flames of hope to brighten
Where despondency had been.
Among my dearest memories
From childhood years that now have fled,
Will be our gathering for prayer,
When it was time to go to bed.
How we always said together
"Gud, som haver barnen kär,"
Kneeling then, you asked the Lord
To keep us always in His care.
In church you have been faithful,
Bringing to my heart a song
Of loyalty to higher things,
Because your faith in Him was strong.
I learned to be at peace, because
You would not quarrel with any man;
If I am honest, your example
Told me not to cheat and feign.

Now my Savior, Christ, has called me
From my childhood home and you;
Gone the days of your protection,
More meaningful than then I knew.
But God be praised, that time shall never
Recollection of those years erase,
When I walked along with father,
Learning of his loving ways.
I on this year's Father's Day
Owe you much I can't repay.
But I want to bring this cheering thought,
That Christ shall be the same alway
We have a future all sublime,
Beyond the realms of space and time,
Where our Redeemer we shall see,
And sorrow nevermore shall be,
O God be praised, He planned for us;
From anxious care we're spared by trust,
He bids us cast on Him our care —
What then remains for us to bear?

❧

Cleansing Rain

March 19, 1978. *Written while Lincoln was teaching middle school students.*

A 12-year-old stands beside me as I sit at my desk. He can't find that city on the map. I hint until we have narrowed it down to about a square inch, and still he does not see it. It is then that I realize that the blankness is not on the map, but in his mind. He can see only that to which his mind is attuned. As important as what you see is what you see with. The eyes of the soul are only half transparent; the other half is a reflection of what we are within. The skies are scarcely glorious through a dime-store telescope.

This is one way of explaining why those who believe in the New Testament God enjoy life so much. He comes down like a cleansing rain, after which the outer world of creation and experience are radiant with that presence.

When I was young, I could not understand how old folks could sit and talk and be content in so doing. Now I know. Not only are the stimuli coming in at a rate beyond what our senses can assimilate, but there is a whole separate world of emotional color, of love, and longing, and loneliness, and above all, grace pouring down. "Behold, I make all things new," he said, and it's true.

Yesterday afternoon I knelt for a long time at the side of my bed. No, I wasn't praying; the bed was the only table surface available, and I was sorting snapshots of the children when they were very small. And I ached inside me; the innocence and trust in those faces got to me, even after so many years. We who are privileged to love others, even our own children, are enriched beyond measuring.

As believers, there is no reason for us to scrape frantically for enjoyment; with a loving God, and people around us help, there is more "fullness of life" than we can handle. ❧

Extend Our Family

Christmas Day, 1988. *A family Christmas letter with a humorous ending: items that are thou* *to be too ambitious are crossed off the resolutions list.*

Dear Relatives:

Dorothy and I have lived long enough now to realize that independence, th quality of life so esteemed by Americans, is actually a very poor virtue wh compared with belonging. It is the group that helps us, not the supposedly de recesses of our own minds.

And it is in the family, God-ordained as it is, that we place much of our hop The extended family, we mean, not only vertical in time, but horizontally as wi as we can make it, claiming its togetherness as a means of living more fully, bo laughing and crying with those whom we claim are within its bounds.

Therefore for the year nineteen hundred eighty-nine WE RESOLVE:

That we shall consider the extended family to be our definition of family – the in-laws, the cousins, the nephews and nieces, plus those we have always called our own.

That our communications shall be based on the Biblical mandate, to "love one another." (*John 13:34*)

That neither time nor distance ought to dissuade us from this commitment.

That since the benefits of our togetherness seem to be in proportion to the frequency of our communication with each other, we will write and phone oftener.

That our main focus will not be on life's trials, but on the positive aspects – health, faith, comforts, and other blessings.

To get the ~~Christmas~~ New Year's cards out on time.

~~To rise each day before 7 a.m.~~

~~To go to bed at 11 or before.~~

~~To keep our phone calls to 10 minutes or less.~~

140

~~To lose weight during this coming year.~~

~~To cut down on snacks between meals.~~

~~To give up chocolate for Lent.~~

~~To save TV viewing for the evening.~~

~~To reply to a letter within a week.~~

~~To get these letters addressed immediately.~~

❧

The Pain of Loving

Mother's Day, 1990. *Prayed during morning worship at Broadway Covenant Church, Rockfo* *Illinois.*

Dear God, I want to talk to you this morning as if I were a child. After all, you and to our mothers we are children still. I want to thank you again, Lord, the mother I had. You remember her; her maiden name was Frida Anderson, a she came from Sweden. Life was so grim for her, all her years. I am glad she entered into rest, and dear God, if you have any special part of heaven for the who had it hard, and yet were faithful, let her be there God. And let me have t certainty she had about You, and your faithfulness.

But all of us here thank you for our mothers. Not just that they were femal and bore children, but that they showed qualities that you describe in the Bib The love, joy, peacefulness, patience, kindness, goodness, faithfulness, self-contr Come to think of it, mothers are worthy insofar as they are like you and your So Jesus Christ. Always trusts, always protects, always hopes, and always persever like the Apostle said.

We hope you can forgive us, God, for the way we sometimes treated o mothers; those years when we knew it all, and thought our parents were hopeles behind the times... when we were ashamed of them. Bless those mothers of ou God, who watched us make mistakes, and still they loved us — something li your love, God. Life has had its revenge by making most of us parents, and served us right. It's kind of a sweet pain, God, when we remember how much th gave up for us to see that we were provided for. Thank you, God, for the moth who tried to warn us how difficult life would be when we were out on our ow Thank you for mothers who trusted us when we did not deserve it; for that moth who pretended not to be sick because we needed her. Thank you that she marri my Dad; reckless, perhaps, but brave, and she never complained.

Lord, it is when we contemplate the whole idea of motherhood that we sen a kind of awe. You must have been there too, God. Humanity doesn't take on no-pay obligation for twenty years or so unless you provide some qualities we do otherwise have. I guess you sat up with mother when I was real sick. I guess ye were standing alongside when they got married. I guess you knew that some d I would come into this world. I know that you're not through with me yet, Go and I pray that your investment in me will pay off.

Lord, we have a special worry about mothers these days. Our nation is persuading them that they ought to take on employment responsibilities too. And it's too much for them. If two incomes means two souls lost - well, God, show us what your will is in this regard. The load was to be easier in our time, and it has become harder. For our mothers who live, give us more love for them; for those who have gone before, give them an extra hug for me... Amen.

Chapter 12:
On the Shores of Eternity

This chapter includes personal tributes to Christians who have gone to their heavenly reward, and writings that contemplate the joy of eternity with Jesus Christ.

Serenity

1994. *Written after Lincoln and Dorothy moved to the Holmstad retirement community.*

Children, be not anxious for the morrow,
Although the path be long with tedious years,
From God, who knows each distant future, borrow
All-sufficient grace to calm our fears;
The Father-heart transmutes our fitful way
Into a timeless, everlasting day.

Children, join to celebrate the morrow,
And let no circumstance forbid the song,
For our inheritance of clear tomorrows
Fills our joyful sight, and quells the wrong.
In jubilant, entranced, untrammeled love
Live out our legacy from God above.

Children, you must dedicate the morrow,
For selves alone are solemn, hollow shells.
Solace bring to those in pain. and sorrow,
Water drawn from God's life-giving wells,
For those who serve this wavering mankind
Shall rapture know, and life eternal find.

❧

Paul Carlson

1964. *Dr. Paul Carlson was a medical missionary who was martyred in December 1964 wh* *serving in the Congo for the Evangelical Covenant Church.*

There was a man to whom the Spirit came,
To tell of lands where hate and sorrow reign,
A stricken place, of misery and woe,
With all too few to lift them from its throe!
He heard! And leaving all his comforts here,
The Master Healer brought his servant near.
What blessed sight to see the rescued stand,
Redeemed in health and heart! There was a man.

When bitter strife engulfed his plain abode,
He knew his task — to stay the blood that flowed.
And even as a captive, radiant, true,
He made his rounds, with faith to see him through!
And then the shots rang out, a martyr fell,
A sound with solemn triumph in its knell;
He died for Christ, and for that needy land,
While millions wept and said, "There was a man!"

Harold Sten

1970. Lincoln commented after Harold Sten died, "He was my closest friend."

He was a granite cliff whose face
was inscribed with Scripture.

He was a rocky headland standing firm
against the waves that broke upon him.

We saw in him a faithfulness illustrating
the qualities of eternity;

A gruffness inadequate to hide the gentle
love that shone out beneath his brow;

The calm solidarity of one whose future is
in the hand of God.

This God-assurance that gripped him was like
a calm, safe harbor to us when we met him.

Like Elijah, he was a pillar firm against new
forms of ancient idolatries;

Like Jeremiah, he sorrowed over the exile of
this generation from its eternal homeland;

Like Joshua, he urged us to choose this day
whom we would serve.

❧

A Soft, Inner Light

1999. *A personal tribute to Lincoln's sister Margaret Pearson Peterson for her memorial service.*

My sister Margaret was a treasure. When we were growing up, I did not know that in a Christian home it is taken for granted that no one gets angry with another, no one carries grudges, no one steals, each one does their job, each one is respectful of parents, and everyone goes to church. Margaret excelled in the qualities that come from the Holy Spirit. I never heard her speak of others except with the love that Christ empowers, and she took her duties in church with utmost seriousness.

Because I am given to song and poetry, I like to razz the people I love in song. But for Margaret, the human frailties were so hidden by her outstanding character that there was nothing to razz. She was outwardly all that she was inwardly.

Margaret's life was somber in her adulthood. It was not her fault. From her father, Ludwig, she inherited a tendency toward depression. She fought it with strong medication, knowing that in her Lord there was reason for joy; but it was a heavy burden to bear. Clarence was the ideal husband to help her fight off the effects of it. Margaret served in the church willingly; enough of the piety of her parents made the tasks seem appropriate and even light. That she became a minister's wife was a natural result. I never heard her complain of the duties of the parsonage, or of the kind of church member that emphasized righteousness but forgot about love.

So I had two sisters who mothered me, sometimes more than a rebellious kid could bear. Helen, who went to her reward a few years ago, tried to teach me to play the piano. My other sister, Margaret, took to the piano with grace, using her gift in church. Margaret also sang alto very well. Her voice was good enough for more than that, but her humility got in the way. I think when we appear in heaven, somebody in authority there will require more of her, and maybe somebody already has.

There is a picture of Margaret and me that has survived; she was five and I was three. Her arm around my neck seems sisterly, but my clenched jaw does not seem brotherly. I am sure there was enough love on her part to make the encirclement seem appropriate, but we little males have so few ways to express ourselves that it was forgivable to show my reaction.

I visualize one occasion when I was playing ball in the street with the other boys on Superior Street; the traffic was not heavy, and we alerted each other to the approach of an auto. Anyway, it was October, 4:00 p.m., the sun shining, but it was getting too cool for comfort.

Margaret appeared on the front porch (home plate was right in front of our house at 3504 Superior Street) holding a sweater for me. She intruded on my athletic musings with a shout, "Linc, put this sweater on. You've got to have more on." At last I heard, "What?" Margie shouted again: "Mom says you've got to have more on." She waved the sweater, "More on; more on!" My teammates saw their chance: "Moron! Moron!" they joined in the chorus.

Margaret fit in everywhere; it was clear to her that what we are, and whose we are, should be apparent. No question of boasting, or making an appearance; I doubt that she ever needed to be rebuked on that score; our worth is that God loves us, and so it was with Marge; the humility that Christianity provides; we are no more than that, but no less either; it never needs to be debated.

I have some idea of who will be here this morning; and that a good number of you have received something from Margaret — something mostly indefinable. As the image of light persists in the human eye and so makes movies possible, so there is fragrance from a believer, and image persisting for a little while after its source is gone. This is my sister to us today; a little bit of something that is a Godly eternity. ❧

The Quality of Eternity

2002. *Originally published on the Internet.*

We seem to be living in a moving vehicle. Sometimes it moves slowly, as in th early years of life; sometime it moves with great speed, as in those times when w long for another moment, but it is not given.

There are times whe, in spite of that movement, we cannot feel that time i passing. Little children, absorbed in what they are doing, forget that the clock i moving, and have to be reminded. Some say that it is because they are newly fror heaven, where the movement does not exist, and have not learned our treadmill.

We adults too find the world standing still in rare moments. A scene so beautif that we cannot absorb it; or a song that comes deeply into us, leaving us with longing, though that song will not do it again.

The moment when the prodigal returns and stands before us - there is heartache that is beautiful, and then time stands still.

There a few adults who never learn time adequately; they are late, and they a surprised that the time has elapsed. That quality, so irritating now, is a foretaste that time when shall resume that other world.

The rest of us long for that horizon. Why do people want to live by or visit tl sea, especially when it is calm? Because that calmness has the quality of eterni Why do we go away by ourselves, into the next room or away from our usu surroundings?

The Sabbath has that quality too; probably it is a command of God because lose our perspective if we never retire from the rat race. Even our wish to sit our favorite chair or pew, and feel that something about it is home, is a univer longing.

There are some old people who give off the scent of eternity. They who h been faithful for seventy years, in work or in marriage; they give off a peace becat something in them transcends the moment, even if it is a piece of a passing a mortal life. The effect of some of them lasts long after their death; that memory a piece of eternity.

The feeling we get by being near eternity is beautiful; sometimes with sadness, as at the funeral; sometimes with joy, as in a reconciliation; Sometime just pure ache and longing; we know what we felt was not of this world.

That feeling has wonderful solidity in it; we are seeing an unshakable kingdom; the ark has come to rest, and the dove has been sent out.

That we cannot duplicate it is proof that it comes from beyond us. If it were only human, then the voice and the key and the occasion can do it again; but no, it is of God.

The sunset, the song, the music, the painting, the voice of a long-lost friend; the face that looked for a second like someone long gone; the forgetfulness of a child, a baby's face that is still trailing clouds of glory; the inevitable longing that comes with that celestial glimpse; God gives us a peek of what will be some day. ❧

Afterword:
Finding and Following
Jesus Christ

What drives Lincoln Pearson to write? Why the lifelong stream of essays, articles, and songs? Behind every witticism, every warning, every word is a passion for the world to come to know Jesus. His overriding desire is for individuals and societies to be transformed by following Jesus, which is often called "becoming a Christian."

What would it mean to "follow Jesus"? How does one become something more than "the very model of a Modern Evangelical"? How might you get "Beyond Church" now, today?

At the beginning of Jesus' public ministry a powerful refrain in his preaching was, "...the kingdom of God is among you." (*Luke 17:21*) "Repent, and believe in the good news." (*Mark 1:15*) The kingdom, as Jesus communicates it, is God's influence, God's reign in the individuals and the institutions of a society. Jesus' proclamation was intended to wake people up to the activity of God among them.

God's activity in Jesus is overwhelmingly good for those who receive and trust it. Jesus said, "I came that [you] may have life, and have it abundantly." (*John 10: 10*) But preoccupation with self undercuts our ability to recognize and live in the stream of God's life-giving love, so drastic measures are necessary.

"Repent!" is Jesus' command to turn from self-absorption and its consequent irritability — "Wake up and turn around!" is a reasonable paraphrase. Jesus calls us to turn from hypocrisy, superficiality, and outright vice. A person who responds to Jesus' call for repentance thus begins a journey of what the Bible calls "eternal life."

Note well that Jesus' greatest anger was against those who presumed themselves righteous. He was amazingly compassionate and merciful toward those who had a realistic sense of their own guilt and shortcomings. If you find yourself stirred to live beyond the superficial, if you feel the tug toward a realistic, humble and mature approach to life, you are beginning to respond to the call of Jesus.

"Follow me!" (*Matthew 4:19*) means in part to trust Jesus' evaluation of the human heart (including yours): "For it is from within, from the human heart, that evil intentions come...All these evil things come from within, and they defile a person." (*Mark 7:21, 23*) Paul, author of a large part of the New Testament, spells it out for us, "all have sinned and fall short of the glory of God." (*Romans 3:23*)

First, admit to yourself and to God any specific sins that come to mind. Facing up to our self-centeredness and naming it is the beginning of health and freedom.

Second, ask Jesus to forgive your sins and set you free from your self-centeredness, a request he is always glad to grant.

Third, live into that freedom by allowing Jesus to rewrite your priorities and principles and even your relationships. As you begin to understand the mind of Christ, you will experience the joy of forgiving and being forgiven, of being generous and living with integrity.

"If you abide in me, and my words abide in you, ask for whatever you wish, and it will be done for you." (*John 15:7*) Immersing yourself in the life and teachings of Jesus will begin to rewrite your life script. Self-indulgence will be replaced by self-giving. Rationalizations and excuses will drop by the wayside, and you will start to develop a character and a quality of spirit you had not dreamed possible. Then you will have not only a new perspective on yourself and your personal relationships, but also more power to love, forgive, and serve.

No Christian, new or seasoned, can afford to go it alone. Christians were made to be among others who are like-minded seeking to mature. Companions along the way are a help, a necessity, and an encouragement beyond words. As you respond to Jesus' call, seek out a local congregation to align yourself with, one that can aid your growth and provide opportunities for fellowship and service.

There is a trajectory to the rebirth of the individual that culminates in the transformation of society—a theme that permeates much of Lincoln Pearson's writing. The reborn soul that is nourished by the Word of God cannot help but band together with other maturing souls to make a society that is increasingly just, compassionate, creative, and free. Thus the people of God are caught up in a life together that sweeps them "beyond church," beyond mere belief, and deep into the presence of the living God.

– Mark Pearson

Bibliography

Books

1. C. S. Lewis. <u>Mere Christianity</u>. New York, NY: McMillan Publishing Company, 1975.

Music

2. Lina Sandell. "Bergen må vika" 1859. Chicago, IL: The Covenant Hymnal, 1950.

3. J. Fredrik Lundgren. "Sabbatsvila" 1884. Chicago IL: The Covenant Hymnal, 1950, 1973, 1996.

Index of Subjects

D

darkness 51
deacon 57, 74
death 42, 47, 48, 66, 94, 102, 115, 120, 150
debt 37
deceit 36
decency 13, 15
democracy 69, 76
demoniac 14, 39
denominations 65, 66, 76
derision 18
despair 124
destiny 121
devil 56, 110
de Tocqueville, Alexis 6
dictator 6, 14
dilemma 12, 21, 28, 74, 75, 77, 84, 100
disciples 46, 66, 83, 92
discipleship 74
discouragement 137
discrimination
  sexual 7
disease 10
disobedience 100
district
  school 23, 24
divinity 64
doctor 105
doctrine 42, 77
drugs 25, 27
duty 18, 36, 59, 119

E

earth 41, 50, 58, 66, 74, 85, 86, 93, 107
Easter 94
editorial 34
education
  Christian 82, 83, 84, 85
  higher 40
  public school 84, 85, 86
secular 50, 80, 110
educationese 20
educators
  Christian 27, 28
ego 48
elders 18
electricity 101, 107
Elijah 86, 147
Emerson, Ralph Waldo 62
emotions 106
empire
  financial 56
  Roman 42, 118
encouragement 154
England 70
envy 36, 118, 119
epidemics 42
equality 56
eternal life 48, 115, 153
eternity 85, 86, 94, 96, 147, 149, 150, 151
ethics 7, 35
evangelicals 38, 43, 55, 56, 60, 61, 77
evasion 20
Eve 100
evil 3, 7, 8, 34, 35, 58, 60, 101, 109, 110, 136, 153
exclusion 45
exercise 50
existence 44
expectations 19
experience 82, 85

F

faith 3, 7, 8, 27, 29, 33, 45, 46, 50, 56, 60, 62, 63, 67, 71, 72, 73, 75, 76, 82, 83, 84, 85, 86, 91, 92, 93, 110, 114, 116, 123, 127, 132, 133, 137, 140
faithfulness 74, 106, 142, 147
fame 44
family 34, 42, 48, 70, 110, 114, 122, 140
famine 10

159

superficiality 153
supremacy 72
Sweden 142
sympathy 42
symphony 69

T

tampering 19
taxes 34
taxpayer 36
teacher 18, 25
  Christian 29
  public school 17, 18, 21, 23, 24, 25
  Sunday School 60, 80, 81, 83, 84
teaching 23, 24, 25, 80, 82, 84, 85
temptation 56, 81
theft 34, 36
thinking
  American 19
  Christian 47
  non-Christian 44, 51
throne of God 31, 55
time 102
Time Magazine 70
togetherness 140
tradition 62, 85
tragedy 102
tranquility 123
travesties 44
trumpeters 69
trust 6, 12, 32, 35, 50, 62, 70, 93, 114,
    119, 137, 138, 139, 153
truth 3, 19, 27, 36, 55, 57, 83, 85, 92,
    104, 114, 128, 136
tyranny 12, 13, 14, 69

U

unbelief 32
unbelievers 45, 46, 76, 83, 84, 105, 116,
    117
union

teacher's 23
  welfare 35
United States 6, 40, 46, 48, 69, 72
unity 69, 71, 82
universe 27, 28, 45
utopia 27

V

vacation 122, 123
values
  traditional 13
vandalism 8
virtue 61, 69
virtuosity 69
visitation
  Christian 48
vocabulary 47
volunteer 34
volunteers 80
voting
  political 36, 41, 66
vows 75

W

Wall Street Journal 5
weakness 56, 101, 119
wealth 44
weight-lifting 50
welfare 35, 70
wisdom 36, 58, 75, 77, 79, 85, 104
witch-hunt 40
witnessing for Christ 29, 45, 64, 82
Word
  of God 56, 80, 85
world view 28
worship 55, 64, 65, 67, 72, 86, 88

Z

zeal 74

Index of Bible References